On Angel's
Wings

On Angel's Wings

JOANNE GULLICKSON

Guideposts®

CARMEL • NEW YORK 10512

"There Have Been Angels in My Life," Hallmark Card.
"Angels Arrive by Ambulance" first published in FATE Magazine (July 1996).

http://www.guideposts.org
Designed by José R. Fonfrias
Typeset by Composition Technologies, Inc.
Manufactured in the United States of America

To my husband, Les Gullickson,
for encouraging me to
write his story.
From his own first-hand experience,
he believes that
everyone has a guardian angel.

Contents

Contents

Contents

~ *Introduction* ~

THIS BOOK IS A COMPILATION of true stories. With the exception of my husband's story, which is the cornerstone of this book, they are published here for the first time. They were written as they were told to me by family and friends. I have tried to keep the tone of each story true to the person that was involved. A very special thank you to everyone who contributed so generously with both their stories and their time. Bless you for sharing your experience with us.

There will be times in all of our lives when we need help. It can come unbidden in the form of a stranger, as in my husband's case, or as a divine being who suddenly appears from out of nowhere to come to our rescue when we least expect it. Angels come in many different guises. Usually, if possible, in one that is most acceptable to the person being helped.

These true stories are about just such moments and more. We hope they will uplift and inspire you, so that you will know,..."You are not alone."

~ *In Appreciation* ~

FROM THE VERY BEGINNING this book seemed to have a life of its own. Therefore, I would like to thank my guardian angel for guiding me with its development.

To Michael Leach, my personal angel, thank you for seeing the potential of the book and your belief in my work. Your referral to Lenore Person, manager of editorial acquisitions at Guideposts, opened the door to publication.

To my editors, Lenore Person and Elizabeth Gold, for your time, energy, help, encouragement and sensitivity. I will be forever grateful.

To my daughters, Bonnie, Debby, Katheryn and her husband Robert, who listened to the stories, made suggestions, gave words of encouragement and most of all believed in me and my work. Thank you. I am truly blessed.

To all those who narrated to me their divine encounters, whether included in the book or not, you made the book yours.

To everyone who helped with this book, I am most appreciative and I gratefully thank you.

With Light & Love,
JoAnne Gullickson

People are wonderful. There is good in everyone. It may be hard to see at times. It may be clouded over by meanness or selfishness. But, within everyone there is an angel waiting to be released.

Robert Schuller
Life's Not Fair but God Is Good

THERE HAVE BEEN ANGELS IN MY LIFE

While they haven't arrived with a blast of trumpets
or a rustle of wings,
I've known them just the same.
They performed their acts in human guise,
sometimes borrowing
the faces of family and friends,
sometimes posing as well-meaning strangers.
You have known them too.
When just the right word was needed,
when a tiny act of kindness made a great difference....
Or perhaps you heard a voice whispering
in a night of sorrow, the words not quite clear,
but the meaning unmistakable,
"There is hope...there is hope."

Angel Arrives by Ambulance

T WAS A HOT TUESDAY AFTERNOON, July 13, 1994, when my husband was involved in a horrendous auto accident that almost took his life. I had been working in my office when he called to tell me he had three stops to make and then he would be home for the afternoon. That was the last time I spoke with him before his life was irrevocably changed.

It was 1:45 P.M. when Les turned off I-17 at Thunderbird Road in Phoenix, Arizona, and stopped for the red traffic light at the intersection. As he sat waiting for the light to change, he was thinking about the three stops he had to make before heading home for the afternoon. The clutch was wearing out on the Dodge pickup he drove, so when the light changed to green, he had difficulty shifting into low gear. As he started to pull out into the intersection, he noticed a movement out of the corner of his left eye. When he turned his head he saw a truck bearing down on him at full speed! He tried to accelerate, but there's not much power in a four-cylinder engine. As he desperately tried to get out of the way of the oncoming vehicle—he was hit! The Dodge pickup buckled like a jackknife, and Les lost consciousness.

Slowly, Les began to come around, but he was in excruciating pain and having great difficulty breathing. Then he realized the engine of the truck was still running. Thinking it could start on fire, he somehow managed to reach over and turn off the key in the ignition. Then he passed out again.

Seconds after the accident, an ambulance appeared on the scene, just as if it had been summoned. It wasn't flashing its lights or running its sirens. It simply appeared quietly from out of nowhere. When it stopped, an emergency medical technician (EMT) jumped from the cab of the ambulance and rushed over to the mangled truck to see if the driver was still alive. When he looked into the cab he found Les unconscious and turning blue from lack of oxygen. His left lung had been punctured by his broken ribs and had collapsed. Not wasting a moment, the EMT quickly administered oxygen to see if he could revive this man who was hovering between life and death. He also gave Les a shot of adrenaline, and within minutes Les started to come around. At least he was semiconscious. The EMT proceeded to check him for other injuries. Les remembers that there was a very nice man who asked him questions about where he hurt. Les later told me that there wasn't a place that didn't hurt.

The EMT told Les that he had broken his left leg. The reality was that his left leg had been crushed from his knee to his hip. The EMT told Les that he would stay with him and hold his leg in place until help arrived. Les also had three broken ribs, a broken collarbone and many cuts and bruises. While they waited for help to arrive, Les continued to lapse in and out of consciousness. The EMT never left his side and continued to administer medical care and encouragement, saying, "Everything is going to be all right. You're going to be just fine." He literally kept Les alive.

All of this was witnessed by the man who was parked behind Les at the intersection while waiting for the light to change. He later became an important witness to the accident. When he saw the ambulance arrive on the scene, he thought everything would be taken care of and, thinking there was nothing he could do to help, he left. He never got out of his van or spoke to the stranger who was helping Les.

Finally, twenty minutes after the accident had occurred, the fire department rescue squad and police arrived. They had been detained by another accident that had occurred at exactly the same time. When the firefighter saw the EMT holding Les' leg together, he seemed surprised and asked, "What are you doing here?"

The EMT replied, "I was off duty and just happened to be driving by when I saw the accident, so I stopped to see if I could help." The stranger then rode to the hospital with Les, never letting go of his badly broken leg until it was safely secured in traction.

When the telephone rang, I knew something was wrong. I had had an uneasy feeling all day and couldn't seem to settle down to work. It was as if I was waiting for something to happen, but I didn't know what. Only six weeks earlier, while counseling a female client of mine, I had told her that I knew my husband was going to have an automobile accident and there was nothing I could do to stop it. At the time I was using it as an example of how little control we have over outside forces or other people. Later, when she heard about the accident, she called me immediately. Since I record all sessions with my clients, this is on tape and can be verified.

As I answered the phone, I took a deep breath and tried to shake the terrible sense of foreboding I had. The voice of a stranger asked to speak to Mrs. Gullickson, and I knew something had happened to my husband. It was a doctor calling from the John C. Lincoln Hospital in Phoenix to inform me that my husband had been in a serious accident. I remember asking if my husband was going to be all right, and then saying that I wanted the doctor to tell my husband that he was going to be okay, and that I'd be there as soon as I could get there.

The doctor replied, "I know he'll make it, but how do you know?"

I paused a moment and then said, "Just a feeling...."

The doctor replied, "Well, he's in a pretty bad way. Drive carefully so you don't have an accident on your way to the hospital."

As I put the phone down I realized I was trembling.

When I finally arrived at the hospital, a nurse tried to fill me in on what had happened as she took me upstairs to see my husband. She said Les kept talking about the wonderful man who had saved his life. Of course I wanted to meet the man, but when she went to look for him, no one could find him. It seems he had left just when I arrived. I asked how I could get in touch with him to thank him, but no one knew his name or who he was, only that he seemed familiar.

When I arrived in ICU and saw Les hooked up to all the monitors, on oxygen and with his leg in traction, I felt nauseous. He looked ghastly, but he was awake and seemed to be aware of what was going on. I smiled, trying to be reassuring. I later discovered that he barely recalled anything that happened after the accident. In the meantime, the hospital was trying to locate an orthopedic surgeon to perform surgery on his leg.

Les went into surgery at 6:30 P.M., and by 9:30 that evening he had been returned to intensive care. Three days later he had to undergo surgery a second time to keep the blood clots that had formed in his lungs from going to his heart and killing him. By some miracle he survived all of this and was released from the hospital eighteen days after the accident.

Les remained on oxygen twenty-four hours a day for seven weeks. Today he is off the oxygen and able to walk. His leg is full of metal, and when he travels, he sets off all the bells and whistles at the airport. But he's alive, and considering what he's been through, he gets around quite well. Thanks to a stranger who stopped to help when he saw someone in trouble.

With the help of our lawyer, we have tried to find the stranger who saved Les' life so we could thank him personally, but to no avail. Our lawyer has talked to all of the firefighters and everyone else who witnessed the accident, but no one knows who the man was who first appeared on the scene and saved Les' life. Our lawyer called all the ambulance companies to see if there was an off-duty ambulance in the area that afternoon. There is no record of any off-duty ambulance being in the area all afternoon—all ambulances were accounted for. Just like the stranger, the vehicle also disappeared.

It has now been four years since my husband's accident occurred. To date we have been unable to find the stranger who helped my husband. He simply appeared when help was needed and disappeared when everything was under control.

Strange? Yes.

Inexplicable? Of course.

We believe that a higher power was at work.

My husband believes it was an angel…his guardian angel.

"Nana, Please Don't Cry"

HERE ARE THOSE AMONG US who believe we are guided to the other side by heavenly hosts. This story is remarkable because there were so many people present when it happened. It was told to me by a very dear friend of mine, Anne Craig.

Thanksgiving had just passed and everyone was in the throes of getting ready for Christmas in 1994, when Grandpa Rags, as he was affectionately called by his family, passed away. It happened so suddenly that it was a shock to everyone, most of all to his wife Nana, to whom he had been married for almost fifty years. Nana couldn't imagine her life without Rags, but she knew she would have to carry on alone.

The funeral had come and gone, but it was after the funeral that life really changed for Nana. She felt as if she was merely rattling around the house without Rags to keep her company or try to tell her what to do, which he loved to do. She felt as if she had to get out of the house. She needed to be around family and friends, so on the Saturday before Christmas she decided to go over to her son's house for a visit. She knew everyone would be busy preparing for Christmas, and perhaps she could help.

When Nana arrived, everyone was so glad to see her that they stopped what they were doing and put on the coffeepot. As they gathered around the kitchen table to chat, it wasn't long before their conversation turned to reminiscing about Christmases past and of course to Rags. As they talked Nana began to weep gently. There were so many wonderful stories and memories about Rags that everyone was laughing and wiping their eyes at the same time. Everyone was touched by the remembrances that came to mind.

As Nana dabbed her eyes with her handkerchief to dry the flow of tears, Megan, her three-year-old great-granddaughter, who had been playing on the floor, stood up and walked over to Nana. Looking at Nana inquisitively, Megan put her little hand on Nana's arm.

"Nana," she said, "please don't cry. The angels took Grandpa Rags. Didn't you see them? When he was sitting in the rocking chair they said, 'We want you to come with us now.' and Grandpa Rags got up and left. He was happy to go with the angels."

For a moment no one said a word. They were absolutely astonished at what Megan was saying. No one had ever told Megan about angels, yet she seemed to know all about them. And it was the way she talked about them, so naturally, as if seeing and hearing angels were the most ordinary things in the world, as if it was an everyday occurrence. They could hardly believe their ears…in fact, they were dumbfounded!

Nana was so deeply touched by Megan's loving words that she stopped crying and dried her tears. It was the first time since the funeral that she had felt comforted and at peace. Now she was certain her dear husband was in heaven with the angels. She also knew, that one day, she would join him there.

———

Wolf, Our Christmas Angel

Sweet souls around us watch us still,
Press nearer to our side;
Into our thoughts, into our prayers,
With gentle helpings glide.

—HARRIET BEECHER STOWE

And God heard the voice of the lad....
And God was with the lad....

—GENESIS 21:17,20 (RSV)

IT WAS LONG AGO when our mother told us this wonderful story about her brother. It was a time of gaslights and horse-drawn carriages. It took place in Minnesota some time before 1920.

It was the week before Christmas, and snow had started to fall early in the afternoon. By three o'clock we knew we were going to have a blizzard of monumental proportions. When my five brothers arrived home from school they promptly headed out to help round up the cattle. All the animals would have to be kept in the barn for the duration of the storm. Everyone was busy doing chores, chopping extra wood, bringing water into the house and doing whatever else was needed in case we were snowbound for several days. To my sister Arlene and me, it seemed rather exciting.

The storm showed no sign of letting up, and while everyone was busy preparing for the oncoming blizzard Mother started to cook dinner. She knew her family would be hungry when they came in from working so hard and they would need a good meal to keep going. There were ten of us, counting Mother and Dad, so we always peeled a peck of potatoes to serve for dinner along with meat and vegetables. Arlene and I had just finished cleaning and filling the kerosene lanterns for the night ahead as mother had instructed us to do. I started to set the table for dinner, which was my job, when Mother told me to go outside and get Fred. My three-year-old brother loved to play outside in the snow with Wolf, the stray half dog, half wolf that had adopted our family. Wolf had been hanging around our place for the past few months, and he particularly liked to play with Fred in the yard.

I took my jacket off the hook by the back door and went out the kitchen door to the closed-in porch. All I could see was the snow swirling around the corner of the house. Across the backyard I caught a glimpse of the barn. It wasn't that far away, yet I could barely make it out. I noticed that my brothers had tied a rope from the house to the barn in case the storm worsened during the night; with the rope they would be able to make it out to the barn in the morning to feed the animals without getting lost. I couldn't see Fred anywhere. I immediately thought he must be in the barn with his older brothers. Not wanting to go out in the blizzard, I put my head out the porch door and tried calling Fred, but the words were caught by the wind and lost. I turned and quickly went back inside the warm kitchen, closing the door tightly behind me to guard against the wind and snow. Mother looked up expectantly.

"Where's Fred?" she asked.

I told her, "I don't know. I didn't see him outside. He must be in the barn with his brothers."

Mother looked concerned. She put down her knife and told me to finish peeling the rest of the potatoes while she went outside to look for Fred. Then she grabbed a heavy coat off the hook and, tying a scarf around her head, she opened the door and went out into the storm.

By now, it was starting to get dark outside and the wind was becoming stronger. The snow thickened against the windowpanes and the wind howled down the stovepipe in the kitchen as my sister and I were trying to finish making dinner. We were almost done when suddenly the back door flew open and my mother and two of my brothers came into the kitchen pushed by the wind and covered with snow. It seems no one knew where Fred or our dog Wolf were. They had disappeared!

The storm was getting worse and now it was almost completely dark outside. My father and three older brothers had lit lanterns and were still out in the blizzard looking for Fred. Eventually they too came inside to get warm. They had looked everywhere on the farm but still couldn't find Fred. They said they could barely see with the snow blowing so hard around them. For the time being the situation seemed impossible. It looked as if Fred was truly lost.

How we managed to get through dinner, I don't know. Dad didn't eat, he drank hot coffee to warm himself as he paced back and forth in the kitchen. Right after they had eaten, my two oldest brothers went outside again with Dad to continue the search for Fred. While they were gone, Mother went to the parlor and got down the family Bible from the shelf where it was always kept. Returning to the kitchen, she placed it on the kitchen table next to the kerosene lantern, opened it and sat down to pray.

It was then that I realized that I might never see my baby brother again. Arlene and I left Mother alone in the kitchen, went upstairs to our bedroom, where it was much colder, and started to get ready for bed.

It was much later in the evening when Dad and my brothers returned to the house. They had not found Fred, and even though they were completely exhausted they were already making plans to look for him as soon as it was daylight. Mother and Dad told all of us to go to bed because we'd need our rest in the morning if we were going to help look for Fred. Tomorrow was supposed to be the day we were going to look for a Christmas tree to cut down; instead we would be looking for my little lost brother. I was so scared, I felt as if I was going to cry.

As I left the room, I turned to look at Mother, who was seated at the kitchen table. She was looking down at the Bible with her handkerchief tightly clenched in her folded hands. Dad, who was standing beside her, put his hand on her shoulder to give her comfort and strength as he looked down at her with both love and sadness on his face. He looked so weary. I felt sorry for both of them, but mostly I was worried about Fred. I wondered if we would be able to find him in the morning.

I don't know what time it was, but something woke me up. Even though it was still dark outside, I got out of bed carefully, trying not to disturb Arlene. We always slept curled up next to each other to try and stay warm on cold winter nights. The wind seemed to have let up, and the house seemed abnormally still. As I quietly crept down the stairs, I could see a light coming from the crack in the kitchen door. On tiptoe I went over to the door and peeked a look into the room. There at the kitchen table sat Mother. She had her eyes closed and she was moving her lips in a soft prayer of supplication. I watched as a tear trickled down her cheek and I knew she had been crying. When I looked at the old clock on the wall I saw that it was four o'clock in the morning. Mother had spent the entire night praying for Fred's safe return. I turned and quietly went back to bed.

The next morning, as soon as it was light, everybody was up, ready to continue the search for Fred. It had quit snowing some time during the night and the sun was starting to shine bright and clear. Wherever we looked there was snow. It was up to the corners of the shed, about five feet high in some places, so there was a lot of shoveling to do to reach the main road in front of the house and clear the backyard.

Just about the time my brothers had finished clearing the driveway, we heard bells. They were coming from the snowplow on Shady Oak Road, the road that ran in front of our house. We watched as our friend Ben, the fellow who always drove the snowplow, pulled up and reined in the horses. Calling out to us in his heavy European accent, he said, "Have ya lost a little boy? Well if ya have, I've found one!"

For a moment it was as if we were all frozen in time. Then we all ran to the snowplow to see what he was talking about. We could hardly believe our eyes when we saw Fred and Wolf in the sleigh. Wolf was wagging his tail and Fred was looking at us in surprise. Words are inadequate to express the joy and relief we felt at seeing our little brother alive. Everyone started talking and asking questions at once. Dad leaned over the side of the sled and held out his arms to his son. Fred's little face beamed when he saw his daddy. As he climbed into Dad's arms I thought Dad was going to cry. He told us to hush so he could listen to Ben, then in a gruff voice said,

"Come on up to the house Ben. You can warm yourself, have a cup of coffee and tell us all about how you found Fred."

When we were all finally gathered in the kitchen, Ben told us that he had found Fred about a mile from our house. It seems that somehow Fred had walked all the way to the corner of Shady Oak Road and Excelsior Boulevard, the road that led into the town of Hopkins. We were all astonished. How did he ever get that far from home?

Ben said that he had started to clear the roads as soon as there was enough light to see. It was while he was plowing the curve at Shady Oak and Excelsior that a movement in the snow caught his eye. We hung on every word as he went on.

"I stopped the horses just as that dog a yourn stood up 'n' started ashakin' hisself. Then I saw what looked like a bright red scarf 'n' a mitten. Well, I jumped down from the sleigh ta get a better look. Folks, I tell ya, that dog a yourn started in a-pushin' his nose inta the snow 'n' diggin' fer all he was worth. Then I saw what looked like an arm of a child. Can ya 'magine my shock—but didn't have time ta think about it. Well folks, I started ta dig inta the snow 'n' there was Fred! He was real groggy. Must'a been sleepin', from what I could tell. I picked him up 'n' put him in the sleigh. Then that dog of yourn jumped in 'n' started a-lickin' Fred's face as if he was takin' care of him 'n' wantin' to be sure he was all right. Well, I tell ya', I ain't seen nothin' like it in all my years. As far as I kin tell, that dog of yourn must'a wrapped hisself roun' your little boy 'n' kep' him warm all night. Saved his life, that's fer sure! Hope ya gotta good bone fer him."

When Ben had finished telling us how he found Fred, Dad, who was sitting next to him, patted him on the back and said, "Good job, Ben. We're lucky to have someone like you around here. You saved our boy's life, and that's for sure. We'll be in your debt forever."

Ben grinned, and Mother warmed up his coffee as she wiped tears of joy from her eyes. Her prayers had been answered…Fred was home, safe and sound.

Mother told Arlene and me to get busy and heat some water so Fred could have a good hot bath. She thought it would help warm him up after being out in the cold all night. Meanwhile, Fred was contentedly curled up on Dad's lap, so tired he could hardly keep his eyes open. Wolf was warming himself by the kitchen stove, and the sun was shining brightly. For now, everything seemed right in our world. This was going to be our best Christmas ever.

Wolf stayed with us for only a short time after the blizzard. It was as if he came to us when we needed help, and once his mission was completed he moved on, perhaps to help some other family with young children.

Was he an angel? To us he was. A Christmas Angel.

The year of the blizzard was also the year of the spinal meningitis epidemic. Fred's resistance had been weakened from his ordeal in the blizzard, and consequently he contracted the illness. While he was ill, he lost his hearing. Later he attended the Fairibault Military School for the Deaf in Minnesota. He became a lithographer and married a beautiful lady named Gladys who was also deaf. Fred was a very bright man and had an extremely active mind. He created many different inventions, some of which he sold. He lived a full, rich life with Gladys...thanks to our dog Wolf.

The night before Fred died he was awake and alert. Even though he had suffered a stroke a few days earlier and was hospitalized, he seemed to be improving. Gladys had just finished helping him with his dinner when he started to gesture toward the air up in front of him. In sign language he asked Gladys what he was seeing. Gladys told him she couldn't see a thing, but she realized that he evidently saw something in the air. Whatever he saw wasn't visible to Gladys or to anyone else. Trying to distract Fred, she asked him if he wanted to come home the next day, but he said, "No," and continued to ask her what was in the air. He became very excited and happy as he gazed into space. He was puzzled when Gladys said she couldn't see a thing. It was at that moment Gladys realized that someone had come to help Fred cross over to the other side.

Gladys was correct. Fred died early the following morning. He was sixty-seven years old.

To this day, Gladys believes Fred saw his guardian angel from long ago before he died.

Angel on the Bedpost

THIS STORY WAS TOLD TO ME by a very dear friend of mine, Dorothy Anderson. It happened many years ago, but it is still vivid in her memory. It reinforces the belief that we are not alone.

When we were growing up, my sisters and I were very close and loyal to each other even though we were each so different. My older sister was quite serious and the best student of the three of us, while my younger sister was quieter and loved to play with her dolls. I was the middle daughter, the tomboy who loved to climb trees and play basketball. Because we were so close, we stuck together and made our own good times.

Our social life revolved around our church activities: Sunday school; church; and in the evening, Epworth League, the young people's meeting. As teenagers we all sang in the church choir.

As time passed, we each married and started our own families. My younger sister Jeanie seemed to be in rather poor health after she had her first baby. Jeanie wanted more children, so she didn't let her health problems stop her from having a second child three years later. It was shortly thereafter, while she was still in the hospital, that the doctors discovered she had a brain tumor.

Jeanie underwent what we thought was successful surgery at the time, but one year later almost to the day, we were told that the tumor had returned. The doctors had been unable to remove the tumor completely. Every year for the next three years the tumor grew back, and every year Jeanie underwent surgery to try to keep the tumor under control. After the fourth and final surgery, her body was just too weak to recover. She had lost her strength to fight.

Something wonderful occurred during Jeanie's last day on earth. My older sister and I had been visiting her every day since she had been ill, but this day was different. She had been drifting in and out of a deep sleep all day, more so than usual.

When the doctor came into her room, he told us that we could talk to her. He said, "She's not in a coma. Talk to her. She can hear you."

I spoke softly to her, asking her if she was sleeping or if she could hear me.

To my surprise she opened her eyes, looked at us and said, "Angels are sitting all over my bed...they're all over my bed. Don't you see them?"

Then she slowly closed her eyes and went back to sleep.

We looked at each other puzzled, then we looked around the room. Of course we didn't see anything that faintly resembled an angel. At the time we thought she must have been dreaming.

It was about nine o'clock when we decided we should go home for the night. Jeanie seemed to be resting well and she was still sleeping. Not wanting to disturb her, I leaned over her bed and gently kissed her good night on the forehead. Irene did the same, and as she did, Jeanie opened her eyes.

"All the angels are gone," she said with a big smile. "Except the one sitting on the bedpost, and he's staying with me."

We, of course, saw nothing, but from the way Jeanie said it, I believed she did.

We waited to see that she was sleeping soundly before we kissed her good night once more, and then we left for home.

It was only two hours later when we received a phone call from the hospital informing us that our sister had passed away. She was only forty-two years old.

Jeanie's death was very difficult for all of us. The loss of our beloved sister was hard to bear and it was a very sad time. I told her husband and their two small children about the angels Jeanie had seen, and how she had told us about them. At the time, I don't know that it helped them very much, but I'm sure in time it will be something they will remember and find comfort in.

As for myself, I know I will. I know my sister was accompanied to heaven that night, by the angel who sat on the bedpost.

Angel on My Shoulder

For a good angel will keep him company,
and his journey shall be prosperous,
and he shall return safe.

—Tobit 5:21, *The Apocrypha*

God is my strong refuge, and he has made my way safe.

—II Samuel 22:33 (RSV)

HE FOLLOWING INCIDENT took place in the early fifties. It happened to my father's life-long friend, Kenny Nelson, founder and CEO of Mama's Cookies.

Why is it that we usually chalk things up to coincidence when we can't find a logical explanation? Often there are unseen forces at work that we are unaware of until much later. When Kenny looked back on that unusual Monday morning, he remembered nothing that would have prepared him for the events that were about to take place.

Kenny was running late as he kissed his wife Charlotte and daughter Merilee good-bye and got into his car. He knew he would have to hurry as he headed for the Miami airport to catch his flight to Minneapolis. That was where his business was based.

He parked in his usual parking place, grabbed his briefcase and bag and headed for the door of the airport terminal. Kenny felt tense as he entered the airport. With his ticket in hand he headed for the gate, his mind preoccupied with thoughts of business. Then a strange thing happened. The thought crossed his mind that he should not get on the plane. He later told my father that he had a funny feeling about the flight. He stopped walking for a moment. He thought he heard a voice say, "Stop, don't get on that plane!" Kenny thought he was hearing things, so he shook his head and continued to walk toward the gate.

The passengers were already boarding when he got there and he thought how lucky he was to have made it in time. Monday mornings were always hectic. Again he paused; he couldn't seem to shake the feeling that he shouldn't board the plane. He thought, *Kenny, you're being foolish.* Then he took a long, deep breath to clear his head and walked up to the boarding gate.

As he started to hand his ticket to the ticket agent, he suddenly pulled it back from the outstretched hand in front of him and said, "I've changed my mind." And without anymore explanation, he turned abruptly and quickly walked away. Hurrying through the airport, he felt as if he couldn't get out of there fast enough.

Once in his car and headed home, he started to relax. He couldn't help but chuckle when he thought about the surprised expression on the ticket agent's face. He had to admit that his behavior had been a little strange. He was puzzled by the overwhelming feeling that something was wrong with the flight. It had pervaded his entire body so strongly that he couldn't ignore it.

Kenny thought about his brother, who worked for him and was expecting him in Minneapolis that day. He would have to call and tell him that he'd take the non-stop tomorrow morning. After all, Kenny was only able to live in Florida during the winter because his brother ran the business when Kenny was out of town. Kenny reached over and turned on the radio.

He was almost home when a special bulletin cut into the radio program. An announcer reported, "Northwest Airlines flight #000 that departed from Miami at 9:30 A.M. for Minneapolis crashed right after takeoff. It is unknown at this time whether there are any survivors. Stay tuned for additional information."

Kenny listened in disbelief. He was supposed to have been on that flight! Shaken, he stepped on the gas. He wanted to get home as quickly as possible—hopefully, before Charlotte heard about the plane crash. He had to let Charlotte know that he was all right. Whatever had prevented him from boarding that flight had saved his life.

Charlotte, who always listened to music as she worked, had just finished cleaning up the kitchen when she heard that there was going to be a special bulletin on the radio. She listened as the announcer said, "Northwest Airlines flight #000 from Miami to Minneapolis crashed on takeoff this morning." He then gave a telephone number people could call to check the passenger list.

Charlotte stood at the kitchen sink gripping the edge of the counter. *It must be a mistake,* she thought. *I must not have heard him correctly.* As she stood there, holding on for dear life, waiting for more information, all she could think was, *Kenny was on that flight! This can't be happening! It must be a mistake.* Suddenly she felt sick.

At that moment, Kenny opened the back door and rushed into the house, calling out, "Charlotte, Charlotte, I'm home."

Charlotte, upon hearing his voice, turned, and when she saw Kenny walk in through the kitchen door, she passed out cold on the kitchen floor.

Later, after she had been revived, she told Kenny that she thought she was seeing his ghost. The shock had just been too much for her.

That evening Kenny called my father to tell him how he had just barely missed being on the fatal Northwest flight at the time of the crash. He told my father, "It was as if I had an angel on my shoulder. It was as if I had someone guiding me, someone who kept me from getting on that plane." He insisted that it wasn't a coincidence. He said that the feeling he had experienced had been so strong, so pervasive, that he had to follow it.

Thank God he did. Kenny lived many more years, long enough to see Merilee grow into a beautiful young woman, and long enough to enrich the lives of his family and friends with his keen sense of humor and love.

The last time my father spoke with Kenny was the night he died of cancer. During their last phone conversation, Kenny mentioned the time he had been saved from death by an angel. He never forgot the miracle that had taken place in his life.

Grandmother's Midnight Visit

*Miracles happen to those
who believe in them.*
—BERNARD BERENSON

"Let light shine out of darkness,"...
—II CORINTHIANS 4–6 (RSV)

I
T WAS DURING THE FIFTIES, when the United States was being swept with an epidemic called the Asian flu, that my story took place. I was a young woman in my twenties.

I had been sick with the Asian flu for a week when I developed a bad cough. While I was sick, my mother and my husband had been taking turns caring for our three little girls. The oldest was only six years old so they certainly had their hands full. We lived in Minnesota and we were in the throes of a bitterly cold winter. The snow and the cold made it difficult for everyone concerned.

I finally went to the doctor. After he had examined me and taken some chest X rays, he wanted to put me into the hospital. He told me I had a very bad case of pneumonia and that the hospital was the only place I would get well. I told him I would take whatever medication he prescribed and do whatever he said, if only he would let me go home. He didn't want to allow it, but he finally agreed to let me go home if I did exactly as he said. He told me I would need to stay in bed for at least a week. Again, I told him I would do exactly as he said. I felt so weak that I couldn't seem to do anything anyway, so it would be an easy order to follow.

I returned home and once there I tried to follow the doctor's instructions. Two days went by, but whenever I got up I felt dizzy and I would start to perspire profusely from the least little exertion. I wondered if I would ever get well. I tried to rest during the day, but it wasn't until everyone was in bed and asleep for the night that I felt as if I could finally rest peacefully. As I moved from the couch to the bed the second night, I wondered if I had made a mistake by not going to the hospital. I finally fell asleep.

I had been sleeping for several hours when I was awakened by a light in the room. I didn't open my eyes at first; I just lay there. Our bedroom was in the front of the house on the main floor, so I thought someone must be shining a bright light into our bedroom window. When I opened my eyes, I saw that the entire room was bathed in a glow, a radiance of almost crystalline white light.

For a moment I lay there wondering what was creating this unusual glowing light in the room. Then as the light continued to become even more brilliant, I sat up trying to comprehend what was going on. I didn't feel afraid, rather I felt as if something mystical was happening. As I put my feet over the side of the bed onto the floor and leaned forward to stand up, I saw her! There was my grandmother! She was near the doorway of our bedroom. She smiled at me with so much love, it is impossible to describe. Then she held out her right arm to me with the palm up, as if she was trying to help me up. I was so shocked to see her that I lost my balance and I fell backward onto the bed. You see, Grandmother had died five years ago. My mother had been ill at the time, and being the oldest daughter in the family, I had assumed the responsibility of planning Grandmother's funeral and the reception afterward.

Not wanting to take my eyes from her, I reached behind me and grabbed my husband's shoulder and started to shake him, trying to awaken him so he could see my grandmother too. He was sleeping on his side with his back toward me. Shaking him as hard as I could, I couldn't seem to awaken him. It was as if he was drugged. I tried again, but I couldn't seem to rouse him. Finally I gave up. Besides, Grandmother was moving out into the hallway and I would lose sight of her if I didn't follow. She seemed to be about two feet above the floor, and she appeared to be dissipating. As she gradually became more transparent, it wasn't as easy to see her.

When I stood up to go after her, she again held up her right hand and motioned for me to follow her. As I followed her into the hallway, she smiled at me. Then, she turned the corner in our hallway. I went around the corner—and she had disappeared! So had the light. She was the light! I stood there for I don't know how long, astonished and somewhat shaken, trying to assimilate what had just happened.

Finally, I turned to go back into the bedroom, and as I entered the darkened room I found my husband still sound asleep. He hadn't moved an inch from where I had left him. As I stood there pondering what had just taken place, I thought, *No one is going to believe me. They're going to think I was hallucinating, what with the fever I've had, and as sick as I've been.* But I knew, I had just seen my Grandmother Schnabel.

As I lay back down in bed, all I could think about was Grandmother. I wondered why she had appeared to me, and why she had motioned for me to follow her and then disappeared.

When I awoke the next morning my cough was gone, and I was amazed at how well I felt. When I took my temperature it was normal! I wondered how that was possible. . . . I had only started the antibiotics two days ago. How could I possibly be well this soon? Then I remembered the visit from my grandmother the night before. Was it possible she had healed me? I certainly felt better since I had seen her.

When the doctor called to check on my condition later in the morning, I told him I was well. He said it was impossible for anyone who was as sick as I was to recover from pneumonia so quickly. "Not in two days," he said, and insisted I come into his office to see him that afternoon. When he had finished examining me, he said that it was unbelievable, but I was completely well. I then told him about my grandmother's visit. He looked at me with incredulity, but said he had no explanation for my sudden recovery.

He did say, "There are some things that defy explanation."

I, of course, believe it was a miracle.

It wasn't until some time later that I realized my grandmother not only healed me, but she had also given me a message. She was trying to tell me that I should "follow her example" in life. As long as I can remember, I never heard her say a bad word about anyone. Rather, she would always defend others in her own nice way. I can remember hearing her say, "He's not such a bad fellow. After all, none of us are perfect." She always treated others with unconditional love.

My grandmother died many years ago, but I will never forget her, or her gift to me when I was a young mother. She not only healed me, but she left me with a beautiful legacy.

A gift of love.

D-Day Angel

There are no atheists
in the foxholes.

—Father William Thomas Cummings

"Behold, I send an Angel before you,
to guard you on the way...."

—Exodus 23:20 (RSV)

ANGELS COME IN MANY DIFFERENT FORMS, as attested to by my uncle's experiences in World War II. He told us this wonderfully touching story many years ago.

My uncle, Warren Schnabel, was a paratrooper during World War II, and was one of the many soldiers who parachuted into Normandy for the invasion of France. At the time, he was in his teens, and even though he felt quite worldly, he was still a young man. Except for his army training, he was completely unprepared for the traumatic experiences of war.

It had been only a few days since Warren's division had parachuted into France and there had been no letup in the fighting. The men hardly had time to eat, let alone rest since they had landed. When the shelling finally let up,

Warren dropped with exhaustion, not knowing if he should try to stay awake or allow himself the privilege of getting a little shut-eye. The night before he had been so frightened, he honestly didn't think he would survive the night. With shells exploding all around him, he had prayed as he had never prayed before for help to make it to dawn. At the time, he thought that he would be better able to protect himself in the daylight.

He must have fallen asleep, because when he opened his eyes, there walking toward him was a great big dog, a German shepherd. Warren looked around, wondering, "Where in the heck did she come from?" One doesn't expect to see a dog walking through a battlefield.

Well, she walked right up to Warren and sat down in front of him as if to say, "Well, here I am. I'll stay with you."

To say he was surprised would be a gross understatement. Although he didn't think about it at the time, it was like an answer to his prayers of the night before. Warren reached out and touched her face just to be sure she was really there. When he did, she licked his hand, and he knew he had found a friend.

"Let's have lunch, girl," Warren said as he opened a tin of food (K rations) and shared it with his newfound friend. She ate so daintily he decided to call her Lady. As he watched her eat, he figured she was probably just as scared as he was. Besides, it was nice to have the comfort of a dog at his side, and at his side she remained.

Lady became his companion all through the war. They crawled through the mud together on their bellies, ate the same food, and at night Lady would curl up close to Warren, keeping him warm during the freezing winter nights. The war raged on. Warren insisted that if it hadn't been for Lady, he never would have made it through the war. Some nights he would be awakened by a nudge of Lady's nose and a low growl if danger was near at hand. She saved his life on more than one occasion by warning him of danger with a bark, growling or stepping in front of him to change his direction to keep him from stepping on a land mine and being blown to pieces.

One night during a battle, Lady saved the lives of Warren and two of his buddies. The men were just settling into their foxhole for the night, but for some reason Lady refused to get into the foxhole with them. She kept pacing back and forth above them, whining. She seemed extremely agitated. Warren knew something was wrong, so he climbed out of the foxhole and went over to Lady to see what was the matter. Every time he tried to touch her and find out what was bothering her, she moved away from him. When he stopped walking toward her, she came back to him and nudged his leg with her nose and then ran away from him whining. Warren followed her.

It was at this point that Warren's buddies, who were wondering what was going on, also crawled out of the foxhole to see what was happening.

"By the way she's acting, she wants me to follow her," Warren said, so the three men followed Lady into the woods. They had only gone a short distance when the shelling started again, and before they could return safely to the foxhole they had just left, it was blown up!! They all looked at one another, knowing full well that if they had been in that foxhole, they would all be dead. Lady had saved their lives by somehow sensing danger. Needless to say, Lady was the hero of the day.

When the war finally came to an end, Warren was one of the first three Allied soldiers to enter the infamous death camp at Dachau. As the soldiers approached the town, Lady stopped in the middle of the road and sat down. Warren turned to see what she was doing, but she just sat there looking at him. Warren called to her, saying, "Come on girl, let's go," but no matter how much he called to her, she just continued to sit there looking at him.

Finally, she stood up, turned and slowly walked away in the opposite direction. It was as if now that the war was over she was going home. Warren watched Lady as she walked away, knowing that she was leaving him and he would never see her again. Then she rounded a bend in the road and was gone. Warren stood there for a moment. He no longer tried to call to her. Instead, he turned reluctantly and slowly entered Dachau.

When Warren finished telling us the story, he seemed to be looking off to some place far away. Then he said, "It was as if she'd been sent to watch over me, to protect me while I was fighting for my country in the war. She was my 'guardian angel'."

Epilogue: After the war, laden with campaign ribbons and medals, Warren returned to his home town in Minnesota. His love of animals had been increased by his experiences during the war and he was never without a pet dog. It's interesting to note that every dog Warren had after the war was called Lady.

Warren died of multiple sclerosis in 1989. He was like an older brother to me and I shall always miss him.

I like to think that Warren and Lady are together again…in a much happier place.

The Smiling Child

The Angels...regard our safety,
undertake our defense,...
and exercise a constant solicitude
that no evil befalls us.

—JOHN CALVIN (1509–64)

For he will hide me in his shelter
in the day of trouble....

—PSALM 27:5 (RSV)

THIS STORY, TOLD BY CHRISTEL LORD, also took place during World War II.

During the war my family—Mama, Papa, my six brothers and sisters and I—lived in Bochum, Germany. Because of its location, in the industrial coal-mining Ruhr Valley, it was one of the most heavily bombed cities in Germany. In just one night a single raid killed thirty thousand people. The sound of sirens going off to warn us of a coming air raid became almost a daily part of our lives. It seemed as if we were under attack night after night and it would never end.

In the beginning of the war our family took refuge in our basement during air raids. There we were able to hear the planes and see the phosphorus bombs as they fell from the sky. They looked like Christmas trees all lit up. We also heard other bombs whistling through the air as they fell before they hit the ground and exploded.

My father was exempt from army service, but he did belong to an organization responsible for looking for survivors after the bombings. It was his job, along with the other neighborhood men, to dig in bombed-out houses and the like, not a pleasant job. Since they were all coal miners, they were more than capable of doing the work.

When the war had been going on for several years, the men decided to dig a bunker. A bunker was like an underground mine shaft, and would be safer than a basement during the air raids. They decided to place it at the end of our large garden.

One night when I was only five years old, the sirens went off as usual. I was so sound asleep under my covers, I didn't hear a thing. My parents hurriedly rounded everyone up to go to the bunker, and since there were no lights or heat on in the house, they didn't notice that I was missing. All of the children had been drilled as to what we were supposed to do. I just didn't hear the sirens.

By the time my family made it to the bunker, the bombs were falling every two meters. It was then that they realized I wasn't with them. My father, who was a brave man, risked his life trying to go back to the house to get me. He was knocked unconscious by the concussion from a bomb that landed near him. He could very easily have been killed.

My mother later told me that everyone in the bunker had prayed very hard that night for both Papa and me.

When the air raid was finally over, there was chaos and devastation all over the neighborhood—our house was the only house untouched! All the other houses in our area had sustained a full or partial hit and had been destroyed.

When my family returned to our house and found me sound asleep in my bed, they said I had a happy smile on my face. I had slept through all the bombing and all the sirens that were going off that night. I had slept through the entire air raid.

My father told me that I had a guardian angel protecting me, and that he was going to go over to the church that night to pray and thank God for saving his little girl. He was a very religious man.

To this day I believe I had an angel watching over me.

Messages from Mother

No one like one's mother... ever lived.
—ROBERT LOWELL

"Do not fear, only believe."
—MARK 5:36 (RSV)

MOTHERS SPEND THEIR LIVES trying to communicate with their children. Those messages can be among the most important we ever receive.

It had been a lazy Sunday, and we had just returned home from a delicious dinner at Mimi's, one of our favorite local restaurants. As I sat down at my desk I noticed the blinking light on my answering machine. Pressing the button to retrieve the calls that were waiting for me, I took a sheet of paper and with pen in hand waited to write down my messages. Then I heard my mother's voice on the tape and couldn't believe my ears. She said, "JoAnne, this is mother calling. I just wanted to check in. I hope everything is fine. Bye now."

To say I was surprised to hear her voice would be an understatement—especially since she was half blind, in a nursing home far away and without a long-distance phone available. She may have had change to use the pay phone, but then she was too blind to see the change or the phone numbers! Besides, she hadn't called me long distance in three years. Her voice even sounded quite strong.

Not wanting to leave the answering machine, I called out to my husband to come hear the message from my mother. He must have heard the urgent sound in my voice because he came to my office immediately. After he had listened to the message, I asked him if he thought it was really my mother.

"Well, it certainly sounded like her," was his reply. Then I replayed it for him again, just to be sure. "She must be at one of your sister's houses. Why don't you give them a call and see if you can reach her."

I thought that's a good idea, but when I called my sisters, both of their lines were busy so I decided to call the nursing home and see which one of them had taken Mother out for the day. When the nursing home finally answered and they had connected me with the right station, the nurse told me that Mother hadn't left her bed all day. She had been in so much pain that she didn't want to get out of bed even to eat. No one had been in to see her because the weather had been so inclement all day. I told the nurse that I had received a phone call from my mother, and I wondered from where she had called. The nurse was emphatic when she told me that it was impossible for my mother to call in her condition. She said that I must be mistaken.

Then to my surprise she said, "Let me go see if your mother is awake."

As I waited, I wondered what in the world was going on. After several minutes the nurse returned and said, "I have your mother here with me so you can talk with her."

Then I heard my mother's weak, trembling voice saying, "JoAnne, is that you?" As soon as I told her, "Yes, this is JoAnne," she continued, "Oh, I'm so glad you called. It's so good to hear your voice. I've been wanting to talk with you."

She didn't sound at all well. I asked her if she had called me earlier, but she didn't seem to understand, probably because I had just called her. She seemed confused and complained about how much her head hurt her. She repeated how glad she was to hear my voice. At that point I said I would say a prayer with her on the phone and she said she thought that would be nice. When I had finished the prayer I told her that I loved her and that one day we would all be together. That was the last time I ever spoke with her.

When I hung up the telephone, I knew she wouldn't be with us much longer. However, I was puzzled by the mysterious message on my answering machine. Evidently there was a much higher power at work here.

While I was thinking about what had just happened, my husband came into my office to see if I had been able to reach my mother. When I told him what had just occurred he shook his head. He couldn't figure it out either, and asked me to play the tape for him again.

When I did, he said, "All I know is that's your mother's voice. I don't know when she called, or how it got there, but it's your mother."

The only thing I know is that she really wanted to talk to me. Perhaps God in His infinite love and wisdom had sent one of his angels to call me on her behalf. I really have no logical explanation, nor does my husband.

By the next week my mother had developed pneumonia. When I called the nursing home to check on her, they called my sister Gloria to the phone to talk to me. She told me Mother was failling pretty rapidly, and they thought she probably wouldn't make it through the night. All I could think was, she would finally be at peace. She had had such a difficult time this last year.

As I waited to hear from my family that evening I busied myself taking care of last-minute paperwork. At eleven o'clock, before I went to bed, I said some additional prayers for my mother and then I retired for the night.

The ringing of the telephone woke me from my sleep and as I reached for the phone I glanced at the bedside clock. It was one-thirty in the morning. My youngest sister was calling from Minneapolis. She apologized for waking me and then told me Mother had died at 11:10 P.M. that evening. Carolyn started to explain all that had transpired earlier in the evening and as she did so, she told me the most beautiful story.

She said there had been a number of people with Mother in her room at the nursing home who witnessed the events that took place. Among them was our other sister Gloria, a niece, a nurse and a nurse's aide. The doctor had stopped by earlier.

Mother was quite uncomfortable, so earlier in the evening they had removed the tube from her throat so she could rest more comfortably. She had been dozing on and off when she opened her eyes and said, "Parents."

Knowing her throat was sore and not wanting to make her talk unnecessarily, Carolyn asked her if she saw her parents. To which she replied, "Yes, they're here."

My sister said she jumped up from her chair to see if she could see anything that was unusual, but then Mother spoke again. She said, "Warren."

Warren, her youngest brother, had died seven years earlier. Carolyn asked Mother what she meant.

Mother replied, "He's here."

It was then that we realized something very special was taking place. Mother was seeing members of her family that were deceased. It was as if they had come to meet her, to help her cross over to the other side.

At this point Carolyn, wanting to help, to make Mother feel better, said, "Let's sing a hymn." When they had finished singing "Jesus Loves Me," they all joined in saying the Lord's Prayer in unison. Then everyone sat quietly around Mother's bed.

Mother seemed to be resting very comfortably with her eyes closed. After a while she opened her eyes and said, "Christ is so radiant." Then she was quiet. When she finally spoke again she softly said, "He's so brilliant."

Wondering what she meant, Carolyn asked, "Do you see Christ?"

Mother smiled and softly replied, "Yes." Then with the smile still on her face, she closed her eyes and quietly slipped away.

As I listened to the story, I thought, *How beautiful. If only we could all leave this mortal plane as beautifully as Mother had.*

My sister and I talked for a few more minutes. I told Carolyn I would call the next day to let her know when we would be arriving for the funeral. There were many arrangements to make and I wanted to call my daughters in the morning to let them know about Grandma's death before I left for Minneapolis. When I finally hung up the phone it was with a sigh of relief. I wiped a tear from my eyes and thought that at least Mother was no longer suffering.

As I lay down and closed my eyes, in the hope of getting a little sleep before morning, I softly said, "Good-bye, Mother, you'll always be in my heart."

The next morning I arose early and called my daughter Debby, who lives in South Lake Tahoe. I hoped she would still be home so I could talk to her before she went to work. When Debby answered the telephone and heard my voice, the first thing she said was, "Mom, I knew it was you. Grandma died last night, didn't she?"

You can imagine my surprise. I managed to say, "Yes, but how did you know?"

"Mother, last night at two o'clock in the morning, I was sound asleep when I heard Grandma's voice calling my name. I knew she was in my bedroom, I could feel her presence. I opened my eyes and I could see a light image glowing. I knew it was Grandma. She was about a foot above the floor and she was slowly moving toward me. As she came closer, I could see her more clearly. She was talking to me saying, 'It was the virus.' She kept repeating the same phrase over and over until I wondered if she meant I had a virus. Then I realized she was trying to tell me that she had died from a virus. She continued moving toward me, and then she reached out as if she was going to try to take hold of my shoulders or hug me, and she said, 'I love you, Debby, I'll see you soon.' Then she moved away from me and was gone.

"It was such a spiritual experience. It seemed unreal, but at the same time I knew it was really happening. That's how I knew Grandma died, Mom. Did she die of a virus?"

I told Debby, "I thought she died of pneumonia, but I wasn't sure." More than anything, I was surprised to hear what had happened to Debby, but I did not doubt her. This was not the first time our family had had this sort of experience.

It wasn't until later, after the funeral, that I read the death certificate. It said the cause of death was viral pneumonia. Debby was correct. Mother had died of a virus.

My mother must have visited my daughter in spirit the last night she was on earth. How else could Debby have known her grandmother had died, or the cause of her death?

Mothers try to communicate in many different ways. I believe our mother was trying to let us know there is nothing to fear in death. Just as she will always live on in our memories, we also believe she lives on in spirit.

Just Like Grandpa

May leprechauns strew happiness
wherever you walk each day,
And Irish angels smile on you
all along the way.
—IRISH BLESSING

"Is your father still alive?"
—GENESIS 43:3 (RSV)

EMORIAL DAY 1996 was a very special day for Nancy and her daughter, one they would always remember.

Nancy had been looking forward to the Memorial Day weekend with her daughter and two grandchildren with eager anticipation. She planned to take them to the Erie, Pennsylvania, zoo to see the animals. This would be their first visit to the zoo. The last time Nancy had been there was thirty-five years ago. She was only twelve years old at the time, and she recalled that it was the year her mother had died and they moved to Arizona.

The family finally arrived for the weekend, and Nancy, along with her daughter and grandchildren, headed out for the zoo. When they arrived, there was already a waiting line to buy tickets. As they stood in line waiting for their turn, Nancy thought she had better check to be sure she had enough money for the tickets as well as treats for the grandchildren. She was surprised to see that they charged an admittance fee for children under five years of age. As she was counting her money, an elderly gray-haired man and woman came up to Nancy and stopped right in front of her. The man resembled her father, who had died four years ago; so much so that for a moment Nancy thought it was her father and was quite taken aback.

Then the man spoke to Nancy: "Excuse me, do you have free passes for the zoo?"

Nancy was still so surprised by the man's similarity to her handsome, Irish father that she could hardly take her eyes off him. Nevertheless, she managed to say, "No."

Then without a moment's hesitation the gray-haired man said, "Here are some courtesy passes for you and your family. They're from the American Legion." And with that statement he handed Nancy enough passes for all of them to get into the zoo free.

As Nancy said, "Thank you" she took the passes, and turned to show them to her daughter Jean. Nancy immediately turned back to thank the man and woman again, only to discover they were gone. In fact, they were nowhere to be seen.

Nancy asked Jean if she minded staying in line to hold their places while she went to look for the nice man and woman who had given them the passes. She wanted to let them know how much her family appreciated the passes, and she also wanted to see the gray-haired man again. Look as she might, she couldn't find them anywhere. They had simply disappeared!

Nancy finally gave up looking for them and returned to her place in line with her daughter. She told Jean she couldn't figure out where the couple had gone.

It was then that Jean said what they had both been thinking: "That man looked just like Grandpa, and what he did giving us the tickets, wasn't that just like Grandpa? It's just the kind of thing he would have done."

Nancy had to agree with her. They talked about the uncanny resemblance to Jean's Grandpa, and also the fact that the tickets were from the American Legion. Ever since Jean's grandfather had been in the service years ago, he had been an active member of the American Legion. What a strange coincidence! The entire incident had an almost unreal feeling about it.

They spent the entire day at the zoo, but they never saw the gray-haired man and woman again.

Nancy later told me, "We'll always remember the man who was just like Grandpa. He certainly was an angel to us."

The Lady in White—A Trilogy

Last night an angel of the God
...came to me.

—ACTS 27:23 (GNB)

She walks in beauty, like the night
Of cloudless climes and starry skies....

—LORD BYRON

HEN I WAS A LITTLE GIRL growing up in Minnesota, there was a wonderful lady who would appear whenever I needed help. She was always dressed in white, and she exuded so much love that I can only believe that she was my guardian angel.

• I •

The first time I remember seeing her I was only about six years old. I had woken up in the middle of the night feeling sick. My throat was sore and I felt as if I were burning up. I hadn't felt well when I had gone to bed earlier in the evening. My sister was sound asleep on the other side of the bed, and the room was dark except for a faint beam of light coming through the open window from the street light. I was thirsty and wanted a drink of water, but I didn't know if I should call my mother or get it myself. Mother didn't like being woken up in the middle of the night, so I finally decided I should get up and get it myself.

I rolled over in bed and looked out into the hallway. The entire house was dark and I knew I was the only one awake. My parents' bedroom was right across the hall from ours, and I could faintly hear the steady rhythm of my father's snoring and my mother's heavy breathing. Everything seemed so still. I didn't feel like getting up alone in the dark.

As I lay in bed looking into the hallway, the room seemed to get lighter…then she appeared! I blinked my eyes because I couldn't believe what I was seeing. There in the doorway of my bedroom stood a beautiful lady in a long, white gown. She seemed to glow in the dark. For just a moment I thought it was my mother, but then I knew it wasn't. This lady was different. There was a twinkle, sparkle, a glow about her I had never seen in anyone before.

Then she smiled at me, and when she did, she emanated so much love that I felt as if I was enfolded in it. I have never forgotten that feeling. As I tried to see her more clearly, she came toward me into the bedroom, smiling at me with so much love that all I was aware of was her presence.

It was then that she spoke to me, saying, "Don't be afraid. I will always watch over you. If you ever need me, I will always be with you." Then she said, "You'll be well when you awaken in the morning. You don't need to be afraid anymore."

I asked, as only a child would, "Who are you? Are you my real mother?"

She didn't answer me. Instead she turned her head as if she heard something out in the hallway. Looking back at me, she put her finger to her lips and then motioned to me to be quiet. She smiled at me lovingly but then she seemed to float backward into the hallway, where she disappeared. All of this happened so quickly that it took a moment for me to realize she was gone.

"Stop! Stop! Please don't go!" I called out. "Please come back. Please don't leave…please."

Just then my mother unexpectedly appeared in the doorway, none too happy to be awakened by my cries in the middle of the night. "What's going on in here?" she asked. It was hard for me to see her clearly and before I could answer, she said, "What do you want?"

The room had become much darker since the beautiful lady had left. My mother asked me, "Who were you talking to?" I tried to tell her about the beautiful lady I had just seen, dressed all in white, who seemed to glow in the dark. I wondered if she knew who the lady was. My mother, of course, didn't understand what I was talking about and told me I must have been dreaming. When I tried to tell her what had happened, she said I had an overactive imagination and that I should go back to sleep before I woke up my sister. She also told me not to bother her again. Then she turned and left the room. I didn't dare ask for a drink of water, but strangely enough, I really didn't feel thirsty anymore.

Long after my mother had left the room and even though I felt sleepy, I lay in my bed thinking about the lady in white. I wanted to hold on to the wonderful feeling of love I had experienced. I wondered who the beautiful lady was. I knew I would never forget her.

When I awoke the following morning I was completely well, just as the lady had said. At the time I didn't think about it. I did wonder about the beautiful lady who had visited me during the night when I was sick. Then I remembered what she had told me, that she would always watch over me…and I knew I would see her again.

• II •

On Angel's Wings

As clearly as I can remember, it was several years later that I had a very unusual experience involving the beautiful lady in white. It was a warm summer evening, and I had been playing over at my girlfriend Beverly's house. Her family lived five doors down the street from us and were like a second family to me. We had been having so much fun playing games that the time had flown by. When I looked at the clock I saw that it was past eight, the time I was supposed to be home. I told Beverly that I had to leave right away because I was late. Saying good-bye to everyone, I left quickly by way of the backdoor. Knowing I was late, and afraid of my mother's scolding, I decided to go by way of the alley even though it was covered with cinders. I thought I might be able to slip quietly in the backdoor unnoticed once I got home.

As I hurried down the back sidewalk to the alley, I heard shouting coming from a neighboring house. The sounds of a woman crying and a man shouting at her at the top of his lungs filled the night air. There was a full moon, so I could see clearly.

Suddenly the backdoor of the house across the alley flew open and a woman ran out, almost falling down the stairs. Before the screen door closed it was thrown open again, only this time by a man wildly swinging a meat cleaver over his head. He came bounding down the steps after the woman. The terrified woman, who was running in circles around their fenced-in backyard, started screaming, "Help! Help! Somebody help me!"

I froze in my tracks. The man—I assumed he was her husband—continued to swing the meat cleaver in a circle over his head as he chased the woman around the yard. The woman ducked behind a large oak tree in the center of the backyard. When she looked out from behind the tree to see if she could see where her crazy husband was, he threw the meat cleaver right at her! Luckily, it landed in the middle of the tree trunk and stuck there. It was while he was trying to remove the meat cleaver from the tree that I knew I had to get out of there.

Scared as I was, I summoned up all my courage, turned and started to run as fast as I could toward the alley, which was covered with cinders. As I started to run down the alley, I felt as if my feet barely touched the ground and it seemed as if I was home within seconds. Once on the sidewalk safe and sound in my own backyard, I heard the voice of the lady in white say, "Go into the house right away."

With adrenaline still rushing through my body, I ran up the walk as fast as my legs would carry me. When I got to the backdoor I opened it as quickly as I could, stepped inside and shut it tightly behind me. Still shaking from what I had just witnessed, I sat down on the steps of the landing inside the backdoor of my house with a sense of relief. It was when I started to brush off the bottom of my feet that I discovered... there wasn't any ash from the cinders on them! It was then that I realized that I had been lifted above the cinders and carried home to safety.

Several weeks later I overheard my mother and Beverly's mom talking about the crazy butcher who lived across the alley. It seems he had been mentally ill for a long time and had recently gotten worse. After the incident, which I had observed unnoticed, he was institutionalized permanently. Shortly thereafter his wife sold the house and moved away. I always wondered what happened to her, for she seemed like such a nice person. I guess I felt sorry for her. In those days, anything to do with mental illness was talked about behind closed doors. It was all very hush-hush.

As to what occurred that night, there isn't a logical explanation. I can only say that I believe it was my guardian angel lifting me to safety... on angel's wings.

• III •

Angelic Intervention

There's a third incident that stands out in my mind during the years when I was growing up. It occurred when I was nine years old. It was a sunny, summer afternoon in the middle of the week, and I had been playing hide-and-seek with my friends in a deserted old house at the end of the block. As we ran through the rooms, the sun filtered through the dust we raised, creating a surreal effect in the room. We had been playing for a while when I had what I thought was a great idea. Without telling anyone, I would go down into the walk-out basement, sneak outside and, when no one could find me, I would surprise everyone by walking in the front door after they all thought I had disappeared.

As I was working out my plan to surprise everyone, I started down the basement stairs, but before I reached the basement landing halfway down the stairway, I felt something brush against my cheek. Thinking it was a cobweb, I tried to brush it aside when I heard a voice saying, "No! No!"

Startled, I looked up from the stairs and saw what I first thought was a fairy. Then I recognized her. It was the lady in white. She seemed smaller to me than I remembered, but I knew it was she. She was waving her arms frantically in front of me as if she was trying to warn me about something. She was so bright it was hard for me to look at her. She continued to wave her arms with her long sleeves (or were they wings?) in front of me. I was so startled that I began to back up the stairs. Then I turned and ran up the rest of the way to the top of the stairs.

When I reached the top, I turned and looked back down the stairs, but my angel was gone. Lenny was standing in the kitchen so I asked him if he had seen her. He, of course, said he didn't know what I was talking about. He then told everyone that I had just seen a ghost. Well, as you can imagine, everyone took off. We were just young enough to be spooked by the thought of a ghost and an older boy telling us we had just seen one (Lenny was four years older than we were). All my friends thought the house was haunted, but I knew differently. My angel had tried to warn me—but about what? At the time, I didn't know.

A few days later we heard that a vagrant had been living in the empty house where we had been playing. Four of the older boys in our neighborhood had found him hiding in the basement and he had become violent. Luckily, they outnumbered him. One of the boys got away and called the police for help. It turned out that the vagrant was wanted by the police for several crimes, and because of the phone call, they were able to apprehend him and put him behind bars where he belonged.

When I look back on everything that took place, I wonder what would have happened if my guardian angel hadn't stopped me from going down into the basement. I don't know....I do know that throughout my entire life, I have been guided by both seen and unseen forces. I may not fully understand what is happening at the time, but it's not necessary that I do. I accept and believe that there is a higher power at work in my life, and in everyone's.

Author's note: This story is a true and factual accounting of what took place. I know, because it happened to me.

JoAnne

Donald's Guardian Angel

NE OF MY CLIENTS TOLD ME the following story about her grandson. She believes he has a very special guardian angel protecting him from harm. From what she has told me, I certainly agree.

When Donald started out for school on his bicycle that morning, he wasn't paying much attention to what was going on around him. Instead, he was preoccupied with thoughts about his dad who had recently passed away. As he approached the corner of a busy intersection, he didn't notice that the light had just turned red, warning him to stop. Instead, he continued riding his bike through the red light—into the intersection and into the path of an oncoming truck that was bearing down on him at full speed.

At the moment when Donald looked up and saw the truck coming at him, he was literally lifted off his bicycle by unseen hands and thrown to safety! The bike continued on its way, right into the path of the oncoming truck.

Donald sat on the ground, stunned. When the truck had passed he looked at his mangled bicycle in the street and tried to figure out what had just happened. He had been thrown with quite a force and as he went over it in his mind, all he could remember was that he had been lifted off his bike up into the air and thrown to safety. It had happened in a split second, and for a fifteen-year-old it was hard to comprehend. Nothing like this had ever happened to him before in his life. It was quite a shock.

When the light turned green, Donald got up from the ground, brushed himself off and went over to pick up what was left of his bicycle. After what had just happened, he was too shaken up to go to school, so he turned and started walking home, half-dragging, half-carrying behind him what was left of his bicycle.

I had gone back to bed after Donald left for school that morning. Just as I was drifting off to sleep, I thought I heard Donald calling me. Even though I thought it was my imagination, I opened my eyes. There he stood, in my bedroom doorway, white as a ghost and looking as if he had just seen one.

I was surprised to see him standing there and asked him what was wrong. When he spoke his voice was shaking, and a garbled story came tumbling out. He told me that he couldn't understand what had just happened to him. When I asked him what he meant, he repeated the entire story again, about how he had been lifted off his bike and thrown to safety. He wondered, since he had been thinking about his father at the time of the accident, if it was his dad who had saved his life, or if it was an angel (our family has always believed in angels and miracles). I told him I didn't know, but that I was thankful that *someone* was watching out for him. Later I told him that I would go to church that evening and thank god for saving his life, and that it would be a good idea if he went to church too.

After his strange experience, Donald was much more careful when he rode his new bike, especially at intersections. Even that didn't seem to keep him out of accidents. Four years later, when he was nineteen years old, his life was spared once again.

Donald was out partying with one of his friends on a Friday evening, when on an impulse, they decided to drive out of town to Canyon Lake. They wanted to see if there was anything interesting going on out there even though it was almost midnight. They had been drinking and needless to say weren't using the best judgment. As they were driving to the lake they missed a curve, lost control of their car and swerved off the road. Their car rolled and fell one hundred feet down an embankment into the dark water of the lake below.

As the car slowly sank into the cold, black water, by some miracle they were able to climb out the back window, which had been broken as they rolled down the embarkment, and swim to shore. Wet, cold and shaken, the two young men managed to climb back up the hill to the road. By now they were both cold sober and realized they should never have gone for a ride after drinking. Knowing there was a ranger's station in the area, they headed out on foot to find it. Luckily, they made their way to the ranger's station within a very short time, where they were able to use the phone to call for help.

When the ranger at the station saw the soaking wet young men and heard their story, he could hardly believe it. Neither of the young men were injured, just shook up and a little bruised.

He said, "You don't know how lucky you are! Last year an entire family went off the road at exactly the same place, and everyone was killed!"

Was it luck? I don't think so. Is there a special reason God has saved Donald's life twice? That remains to be seen…only time will tell.

As for Donald's grandmother, she believes her grandson has been protected by a guardian angel all of his life, and as I said in the beginning, I would have to agree with her.

Seeing Grandma Again

JUDY LEACH TOLD ME this amazing story. "Today when I think about what happened to me, it is as clear in my mind as if it happened yesterday."

In the spring of 1970 the most incredible experience of my entire life took place. For a long time I thought it was only a dream. It began when I was five months pregnant with my second child. I had been having problems with the pregnancy from the beginning and I had a feeling that something was terribly wrong.

My doctor, Dr. Morrisey, who had delivered my daughter five years earlier, was like a friend to me. Because I knew him so well, I trusted him and had confidence in his ability as a doctor. The week before, I had been to his office for an examination. It was at that time that Dr. Morrisey told me that he was unable to detect the baby's heartbeat. Even though I had known something was wrong, I was heartbroken to learn the baby had died. Dr. Morrisey tried to prepare me for what would happen next. He told me that I would go into labor soon and when I did I should call him right away.

When labor started the following week, I immediately called Dr. Morrisey, and we agreed to meet at the hospital at 3:00 P.M. where I would be admitted for observation. Shortly after I was admitted, Dr. Morrisey arrived and told me they were going to prepare me for surgery. He reassured me that everything was going to be all right, and that he was going to perform a D and C (dilation and curettage) on me. He also said that I would be able to go home forty-eight hours after surgery. (Remember, this was 1970, or I probably wouldn't have survived. Today patients are sent home the same day as surgery.)

After surgery was completed and I was settled in my room, I recall feeling that I was tired but glad it was over. I looked at my watch and remember that it was about 9:00 P.M. when I fell asleep. At some point during the night I awoke and felt that something was terribly wrong, but I didn't know what. Then I remembered there was a button behind my head to call the nurse. When I reached for it I couldn't seem to find it, but I really didn't care. In spite of that, something made me search until I eventually found the button. It seemed as if it took every last ounce of strength I had. That's the last thing I can remember.

The next thing I knew, I was flying rapidly up a black tunnel toward a white light. I felt as if I was experiencing something over which I had no control. I remember feeling frightened and wondering what was at the end of the tunnel where the light was. As I continued to move faster toward the light, I felt as if hands were trying to grab me. I didn't know what was going to happen to me or what I was going to find when I got to the end of the tunnel. I was scared.

Suddenly, I was at the end of the tunnel and I was in the light. Everything was so peaceful and calm. When I looked around I saw fluffy clouds and flowers, white and gold. It was almost like a pastoral scene in the distance. Then, the most surprising thing of all—I saw my grandmother standing there!

She was just as I remembered her in life, except that she was dressed all in white. Sitting next to her was my beloved dog Snapper, my constant companion who had seen me through all of my childhood years. I was fifteen years old when Snapper died of old age, and oh, how I had missed him. Now, here he was with my Grandmother Gregg, and even though Snapper was sitting down, his tail was wagging back and forth as fast as it could go. Snapper was looking at Grandma with such love. He obviously loved her very much and I knew he wanted me to know. It was as if he had found the perfect companion.

My grandmother had died the year before in a tragic auto accident. And, as so often happens in life, I didn't realize how much I loved her or how much I would miss her until after she was gone. Now, here she was right in front of me.

I reached out to her with my arms outstretched, wanting to get as close to her as possible. But, as I moved toward her, she put out her arm with her palm facing me and said, "Stop!" in a firm voice.

I stopped immediately and replied, "Oh, Grandmother, I'm so happy to see you again and to know that you're well." I continued to reach out to her, trying to bridge the distance between us.

"Stop! Stop!" she said. "You mustn't come any closer or you'll have to stay here."

I was completely puzzled by her reaction and her words. When she sensed my dismay she began to explain it to me: "If you touch me, then you'll have to stay."

"But Grandma, I want to touch you. I want to stay with you, to be with you." I felt as if the longer I was in the presence of my Grandmother Gregg, the more attached or connected I became to her.

It was at this point she reiterated, "No! No! You must go back! It's not your time yet. You're young and you have a husband and a child to raise. They need you." She continued, "When you come again, I will still be here. Your dog will be here too. There will be time to stay and visit. We will be waiting for you— but it's not time yet. You have things to do on earth."

I wish there were words to express how bewildered I was by her words and how sad I felt because I couldn't touch her. I thought to myself, *I just got here and now you're sending me away.* I felt completely bereft of her love, and to make matters worse, I was afraid I would never see her again. In my mind's eye I saw myself crying. I didn't want to leave her or Snapper or such a beautiful place.

Then, as if she was reading my mind, she said, "Please don't feel so badly. You'll understand in time. Please, go back now!"

The next thing I recall, it was morning. When I opened my eyes the sun was streaming through the hospital window and Dr. Morrisey was standing beside my bed.

"Well, hello there, young lady," he said. "I don't think you realize how lucky you are to be here this morning. We almost lost you last night. I've been sitting here ever since they called me last night to tell me you were bleeding internally. I don't know how you had the strength to summon the nurse."

He went on to say, "I've called a gynecologist to examine you to be sure you're all right. You don't know how fortunate you are to be alive. You were bleeding internally for hours and I wasn't sure we could save you. You're going to have to stay here for at least a week and then take it easy for a while when you go home." He asked me if I would be okay if he went to look for the doctor he had called, and when I had reassured him that I thought I would, he left the room.

It was nine days before I was released, and I was admonished to stay off my feet for at least another ten days when I got home.

I repeatedly thought about what had happened that night in the hospital.

Assuming it was merely an overactive imagination, I came to the conclusion that my visit with my grandmother had just been a dream. It wasn't until several years later that I realized I no longer had any fear of death.

It was in the eighties when I first heard Dr. Raymond Moody speak on television about NDEs or "near-death experiences." That was when I realized that what I had experienced that night in the hospital was, in fact, a "near-death experience." No one can convince me otherwise.

I have kept the memory of my grandmother waiting for me in my mind. It is as real to me today as the day it took place. I find it reassuring to know that we will be free of infirmities and well in spirit when we leave this earth. It is also comforting to know that someday we will be reunited with those we love who have gone on before us, to the next dimension.

Mother's Gift

"Where there is no darkness, nor
sorrow, nor death...and my mother
is there...and my Savior is there;
...I hope that I shall be there too."
—ELIZABETH WETHERELL, *The Wide, Wide World*

If there be for him an angel....
"let him return to the days of
his youthful vigor...."
—JOB 33:23,25 (RSV)

THE FOLLOWING STORY was told to me by a professional golfer. Her life was dramatically changed as a result of this unusual experience.

The funeral was lovely, but my sister and I felt a sense of relief when it was over. When our mother died on November 19, 1990, we knew she was finally free of the pain she had endured for so long. We knew we would miss her terribly. She had always been important in our lives, even when we became adults, and now she was gone.

We decided to stay on at Mother's house after the funeral, sharing the guest bedroom just as we had shared a room when we were growing up. We had many things to accomplish in the next few days, and staying there made it easier.

When we went to bed the night after the funeral we were both exhausted, and we fell sound asleep almost immediately. It seemed as if we had only been sleeping for a short time when something woke us. I looked at the clock on the dresser and it was 3:33 A.M. It was then I realized that there seemed to be a presence in the room with us. I looked over at my sister, and she was also awake. She motioned to me not to say anything. We both sensed that something or someone was in the bedroom with us. Was it a ghost? A spirit? Was it possible it was Mother? We couldn't tell, but we knew we weren't alone. We waited for something to happen, but nothing did. Eventually, whatever was there seemed to dissipate, and we fell back to sleep.

In the morning we discussed what had happened during the night and we both wondered who or what it was that had visited our room in the wee hours of the morning. Neither of us had an answer.

After a busy day of trying to organize and take care of everything for Mother's estate, we once again retired for the night. At this point we were too tired to even think about the events of the night before, and in a matter of minutes we were sound asleep.

Then it happened again. Something awoke both of us. When I checked the time, it was exactly 3:33 A.M., the same time as the night before when we had been awakened, and again there was a presence in the room. We didn't feel uncomfortable nor did we feel that we were in any danger. Rather, the feeling in the room was one of peace and tranquility.

As we lay in bed waiting to see if anything unusual was going to happen, we drifted off to sleep and didn't awaken until morning. Once again we talked about our nightly visitor, but since we were leaving the next day, we had to get down to the business at hand and we soon forgot all about it.

It was late when we finally went to bed the last night. Mother's house was going to be put on the market and sold, so we knew it was the last time we would ever stay there. We both felt we were saying a final good-bye to our mother and our childhood.

I tossed and turned, unable to go to sleep. Perhaps I was overtired. I must have dozed off because suddenly I was awakened by the presence of someone in the room. I lay there mystified, yet absolutely certain that someone was sitting in the rocking chair! Although I couldn't see whomever it was, I knew someone was there. I felt the hair on the back of my neck start to stand up. I looked over at my sister, who was wide awake. We both sat up and looked around the room. The presence in the room was much stronger than it had been the two previous nights. I glanced over at the clock. It was exactly 3:33 A.M.

Then we heard a voice say, "God will make you whole."

We no longer felt afraid. We knew it was our mother. Her favorite fragrance filled the room. I can't describe the feeling of love we experienced...it was true joy.

Now we knew for certain that Mother was free from all suffering and in a place filled with love. What we didn't understand was the meaning of her message, or the impact it would have on us. After this incredible experience, this visit from our mother the last night in her house, we knew she would always be with us in spirit.

As my sister and I said good-bye to each other the following morning, we felt reassured that life definitely does go on.

Only two weeks after the visit from our mother, my sister Karen, who had been crippled from a stroke several years earlier, was miraculously healed! She had worn a leg brace constantly since the stroke, but after returning to her home she was able to take the brace off and throw it away. She has never worn it since.

As for myself, I was guided to make some decisions about my career and my personal life that helped me find my true path. I went to work for the L.P.G.A., setting up golf schools for children. Five have been opened in Florida with more to come in other states. My new career has given me the opportunity to help others; my life has been truly changed for the good.

My sister and I believe it was our mother who guided and helped us. I know her spirit will always be with us.

The Visit

*A good portrait is a kind of biography, and neither painter nor biographer
can carry out his task satisfactorily unless he be admitted behind the scenes.*
—ALEXANDER SMITH

And a vision appeared to Paul in the night...
—ACTS 16:9 (RSV)

HIS STORY WAS WRITTEN by my friend, Bruce A. Swinton. It confirms the belief that life goes on after death.

The Picture (Window)

"Who is that man in the picture, Daddy?"

How many times as a child I must have asked that question as I stood staring at the picture in my grandparents' front room. A studio portrait probably, in an eight by ten frame, maybe taken years earlier for a high school yearbook. The straight-on pose seemed almost clinical, and the photo's background nothing more than white streaking dots on a black canvas. The subject appeared to be lit by a car's headlights in a nighttime winter blizzard.

I was always drawn to the photo...even "called" by it, as strange as that may sound. Yet, as I gazed at it, the photo was almost disturbing, for it seemed more than just a picture in a frame. More like a window, with a man looking in on us as we grew up year after year. He was a young man, eighteen or nineteen maybe, with a chiseled jaw and Gable good looks. His expression was pleasant but distant—not your typical photo smile. There was something more in his silent stare. It almost seemed as though he knew something when that flashbulb popped, a secret or a vision that he couldn't express or share with anyone. At least that's what it seemed like to my young mind as I stood gazing at the man in the picture.

"Who is he, Daddy?" I asked again.

"Why that's your Uncle John, as I told you before," my father would reply.

"Where does he live, Daddy, and why don't we ever see him?"

"Because, son, your Uncle John lives in Heaven with Jesus. He died years ago, before you were even born."

"Did Grandma know Uncle John, Daddy?" I inquired.

"Why sure, son, Grandma knew him very well."

"I'm going to ask Grandma to tell me about Uncle John," I proudly stated as I began to march off.

With a startled look on his face my father said, "Please don't talk to Grandma about it right now, son. Why don't you go outside and play for a while."

It made no sense to me. He was my uncle and his picture was in my grandparents' home but we couldn't talk about him. To a curious young boy it only raised more questions. How did he die? Why did he die? Was he sick? Was he hurt? Questions that would only be answered many years later, and only after gazing at the man in the picture (window) many more times…all the while knowing not to talk about the man or the picture with Grandma.

My Search

When I was sixteen or seventeen I decided it was time that I learn some answers about my Uncle John. By that ripe age I was convinced that I had all of the answers to life's riddles, so why not his? But this time, I wouldn't ask my father and I certainly couldn't ask my grandmother. This time I would go to Mom with my curiosity. My search for the facts could now end, and I would know how I had lost an uncle that I had never known.

A Night Remembered—Mom's Story

My older sister Donna was just a newborn the weekend my folks arrived with her in my grandparents' driveway for a weekend visit and a family reunion. Two proud new parents would show off the first of what would eventually be seven children. Baby Donna would coo to her grandparents and giggle at her Aunt Ellen, who was only a teenage girl at the time. And for the first time she would meet her Uncle John. He was finally back home in that small, northern Iowa town, home from years of honorably serving his country in the military during World War II. But more recently, he was home from touring all forty-eight states in the union with his three service buddies. What stories the four of them must have had to tell that weekend!

It was probably a typical homecoming atmosphere in that small midwestern farmhouse; the aroma of apple pies baking in the oven; chickens readied to be fried; and lots of love and laughter all around. After dinner everyone probably moved out to the back porch and visited to the whine of the stock car races at the county fairgrounds a couple miles off.

Then suddenly Uncle John had an idea. How many years had it been since he had been to a Saturday night dance at the ballroom in Janesville? They would all go over there to the dance.

"Come on, Wendell," he begged my father. "You and Carol are coming with us!"

My mother made it clear very quickly that she certainly was not going anywhere when she had this young one to take care of.

"Wendy, you go with the boys. I really think it would be good for you and John to spend the time together," my mother said.

But as much as she insisted, that much more he declined. She had never seen him respond so adamantly.

"The boys can go to the dance without me. I'm staying here!" my father informed her.

It was a decision he would anguish over for years to come. Many times my father thought that maybe if he had gone with them that night, the young men would have made it back home safely. But they did not....

As my mother recalls, it was around 5:00 A.M. when they were awakened by the dog frantically barking in the yard. Shortly after came knocks on the back-door. Mom can't recall now who actually made it to the door first to greet the sheriff and his deputy, because almost immediately, for her and for everyone in that house that early dawn, the world turned upside down. It was as if things began moving in slow motion and fast forward all at the same time.

"We believe your son died instantly and without pain," the officer informed my grandparents. "His two buddies in the back seat didn't survive, but the other young man, Zeke, appears to be uninjured."

My uncle had apparently fallen asleep behind the wheel as the car approached a bridge. The car collided with the bridge and went over the side. My uncle's body was found several yards downriver from the vehicle.

My mother recalled to me the grieving beyond measure that flooded the family, as well as the whole farmland community. My grandfather had always been a sensitive and emotional man. The news of his young son's death nearly flattened him. Mom remembered how strongly my grandmother dealt with the news as well as all of the arrangements to be made for her son's funeral and burial. Her strength was almost frightening. As her boy was lowered into the earth, and those nearby were wracked with sobbing, she shed not a tear. She appeared to be untouched by the events that were taking place.

As I listened to my mother's words, it became clear to me why we had always been instructed not to talk about Uncle John in my grandmother's presence. Perhaps she had never gotten over his death and just couldn't speak of her son. I didn't know exactly, but I knew I wouldn't be satisfied until I could one day speak to her about it.

The Courage to Ask

One weekend I decided to head over to the small town where my grandparents lived and stop by to see them. After a wonderful farm-style lunch we moved into the living room to visit. As I sat across from Grandmother I noticed that Uncle John's picture sat on the table beside her chair. As the conversation turned toward family and days gone by, I finally built up the courage to ask Grandmother about that fatal night when my uncle died. As she told me the story, the tears began to well up in her eyes. I told her that if it was too painful, we didn't have to talk about it. I said that's why I never brought it up before. However, the words she spoke then made me wish I had asked many years earlier.

The Visit

"He came to me, you know," she said as she cleared her throat. "It was in the night. Oh, I know that for years the others have probably told you not to talk to me about this, but don't you see, none of them know that he paid me a visit one night!"

"Who paid you a visit?" I asked, fearful of the answer I might receive.

"Your Uncle John," she replied, "a few nights after he died."

So this was why I had always been told never to bring up the subject of his death. Evidently, she was delusional and maybe even a little crazy from her grief. She soon made it clear that she was neither.

"They probably told you how strong I was when he died. Didn't they? Told you I never shed a tear, right?" she asked. "They were all fooled, you know...I wasn't strong at all. I was just in denial. You see, when that sheriff gave us the horrible news about John, I absolutely refused to hear him. My mind couldn't believe it. When the door was opened and I saw the uniforms I think I already knew what the words were going to be. From that moment on, I convinced myself that none of it was true...just couldn't be true. Everyone commended me on how strong I had been through the funeral, but it was only because, in my mind, your uncle was still very much alive, and none of this was really happening. I went on that way, denying it, not believing it had really happened, not until he paid me a visit one night."

I may have been sitting there with my jaw dropped open, I don't know, but I was beginning to believe what she was saying.

"It was one night maybe five or six days after we buried him. I had hardly eaten or slept in over a week. I lay there tossing and turning, wondering how I was going to face another day, wondering when this awful nightmare would end. It was then, near the foot of the bed, that there started to gather some kind of light. At first, it was just like the beams you see after you've looked at something too bright. I thought I was starting to see things. Hallucinate, you know—from my lack of sleep. But then...there he was, all at once, inside these light clusters...and he was smiling at me. I sat up, I went to reach for your grandfather, but it was as if my hands had weights on them. I tried to speak and I was mute. I blinked several times, thinking the illusion would clear. Then he began to speak.

"'I'm all right, Mother. We have to say good-bye now. You have to let me go. I'm going to be fine,' were the words he spoke."

Grandmother continued, "Then as quickly as he had come, he left. It was when I tried to call for your grandpa that a horrible, yet wonderful sob rose from my throat. I felt my cheeks and there were tears. I lay back on that bed and cried. Really cried. Cried for days without stopping. Sometimes because I was so miserably sad, and other times because my son was going to be fine and it made me so happy. But nonetheless, I had said good-bye and I had let go."

Once more, tears streamed down her cheeks.

Appreciation

Uncle John, we never met, and yet you have always been there in your window, looking in on us. I searched to know you through the tales of others, but I still feel cheated. I don't know what your life would have held had you lived longer, but I do know one thing for certain. You gave your mother a very special gift, the gift of healing. You made her able to move on past your death and her grief, so she could concentrate on the good in life.

Uncle John, you must have been a good man. If you can hear me right now, thank you for the gift you gave my grandma. Thank you for the visit.

The Christmas Star

A very happy Christmas day was that.... Young and old dined together today,
and the children not set by themselves....

—Elizabeth Wetherell, *The Wide, Wide World*

"Let light shine out of darkness,"...

—II Corinthians 4:6 (RSV)

A DEAR FRIEND OF MINE, PATRICIA E., told us this beautiful story about her niece, and a Christmas gift she will always remember.

It was Christmas Day, and we had spent the holiday with our family over at my sister's house. All the relatives were there and what a wonderful time we had, being with those we loved during the holidays and sharing the joy that abounds at that very special time of the year.

However, I noticed that my sister's daughter Debbie seemed more quiet than usual. She had taken the death of her grandmother this last year very hard. Debbie and her grandmother had always been very close; they seemed to have a very special bond.

Finally, as all good things do, the day came to an end and we had to part. It was about 11:00 P.M. when we finally said good-night to everyone and headed home. On the way I couldn't help but think about Debbie. She had seemed so down when she left, and it wasn't like her. She was usually so happy on the holidays. Debbie is truly one of the most kind-hearted persons I have ever known. She took care of a number of pets including my father's two dogs. She would always stop to help a stray animal in trouble, and she usually ended up taking them home to live with her. Her pets were her family.

Several days later, she told us this story.

Debbie drove home alone that night and thought about the beautiful day she had shared with her mother and dad and all the relatives. She had to come to grips with the fact that she had been feeling lonely ever since her grandmother had died. How she wished she was married and had her own family!

Once inside her home, even though it was late, Debbie put on her robe and laid down on the couch in the living room across from her Christmas tree. As she wrapped her robe more securely around herself, two of her cats, Jasmine and Spankey, jumped up on the couch and curled up beside her, while the dogs laid down on the floor next to the couch.

Now that she was alone, even with her pets around her, she really felt blue.

As she looked across the room at the Christmas tree, she realized she had forgotten to turn on the lights. But then, since there was no one there to share it with her, she decided not to bother.

It was at that very moment that the star at the top of the Christmas tree began to glow!

Debbie blinked her eyes; she thought she must be seeing things. Then the light went out just as mysteriously as it had come on.

There must be a short in the wire to the lights, she thought, and then she remembered that she hadn't even plugged the lights into the electrical socket.

Then, just as before, the star started to glow again. It continued to blink slowly on and off, on and off, for about ten minutes. Debbie never moved. She couldn't take her eyes off the star at the top of the tree.

Then she started to smell a familiar fragrance and sense a feeling of love. A warmth surrounded her and she knew that she was not alone. It was her grandmother! Debbie felt as if her grandmother was speaking to her, telling her that she was with her, that she would always be with her, watching out for her. Debbie could feel her grandmother's love. But more importantly, she felt a peace and contentment she hadn't felt since her grandmother's death.

The next morning when Debbie called her mother she was so excited that the words literally tumbled out of her mouth. She told her all about what had happened the night before and said she felt better than she had in a long time. She felt as if she had been renewed.

When Debbie told me this story, tears of joy and wonder filled her eyes. She said, "I know it was Grandma. She wanted to let me know that she was with me, that I wasn't alone. I know this sounds crazy, but it really happened, and I'm truly happy for the first time since Grandmother died."

Then softly she said, "I know I'll never be alone again."

Angels have appeared to countless men and women throughout the ages. Usually, it is in times of despair. Whether it was Debbie's grandmother or her guardian angel who healed her spirit, who can say. All I know is that a wonderful transformation had taken place in my niece.

It was truly the loveliest Christmas gift we received that year.

Arizona Angel

Many times an angel will take on the form of a person and be mistaken for a human being. This story comes from Sara O'Meara.

My husband Bob and I, along with our good friends, Yvonne and her husband Don, had just finished helping our daughters settle in at Arizona State University. It was their first year away from home at college so we wanted to make sure that everything was okay. After saying our good-byes we immediately started out on our trip back home to Los Angeles, and this is where our real adventure began.

As we headed out of Phoenix, we stopped at one of those all-service family gasoline stations for cold drinks and ice to take on the trip, as well as a tankful of gas. When we were ready, we climbed back into the van and made ourselves comfortable for the long trip home. Yvonne started out driving.

We had been traveling for some time when Bob said, "I thought the sun set in the west!"

I'm the world's worst when it comes to directions and hadn't noticed that we were going in the wrong direction. It seems that Yvonne had taken a wrong turn when we pulled out of the filling station and we had been driving east instead of west for the last hour and a half. When we finally figured it out, we turned around and drove back in the direction from whence we came.

When we finally pulled into the same old gas station we had visited at the start of our trip, the man there asked, "Didn't I see you in here before?"

You can imagine how silly we felt. We had been traveling for three hours and we were back in the same place where we had started. We looked at one another and laughed. What else could we do?

Once we were straightened out in our directions, we headed out again and all seemed to go well for a while. We had been traveling on I-10 for what seemed forever, when we heard a *thump, thump, thump*. We had a flat tire! Here we were, out in the middle of nowhere, and now our van had a flat. What next!

There were no other cars on the road. Every now and then a truck would whip by us, sending up swirls of dust and making our van shudder as if it were a piece of paper. Realizing there was no one to help us, we decided we had no choice but to change the tire ourselves. This involved unpacking the entire back of the van because the car jack and the spare tire were at the bottom of everything. To top that off, Yvonne and I had packed our clothes in plastic bags, which lent themselves to being blown across the desert scenery! We chased after them for at least fifteen minutes in order to retrieve our belongings. In the meantime our husbands struggled trying to fix the flat tire with a very inadequate jack. Hot and tired, Yvonne and I returned to the van with our belongings, only to find that Bob and Don had been unable to jack up the van.

It was at this point that I said, "We'll just pray for someone to help us. We'll pray for someone to stop."

Don responded with, "No way will they stop. With the speed of the trucks they couldn't stop if they wanted to, or they might be hit."

Everyone was quiet. I silently prayed for help.

Not much time had gone by when we saw a funny-looking truck out of yesteryear come chugging down the road. You can imagine our surprise when it pulled up right behind us. A little man with only one tooth appeared from the cab of the truck. Yvonne was so fascinated with his one tooth that she didn't really listen to what he was saying. We told him about our problem and asked him if he would be so kind as to call for someone to come out and help us when he reached his destination.

He quickly replied, "No need for that. I have a hydraulic jack in the back of my truck."

You can imagine our astonishment!

The little man went back to his truck and took out the jack. We all looked on in amazement as this little man who, with no help from us, lifted our car with one press of his foot on the jack and then replaced the tire.

The four of us stood there admiring his miraculous handiwork, but to our astonishment, when we looked up to thank him, we discovered both he and his truck had vanished. Surely we would have noticed if he had driven by us. We would have seen him. We looked back and forth in both directions on that long stretch of open highway and there wasn't a sign of him anywhere. He had quite simply, disappeared!

Don and Bob looked at Yvonne and me, and in unison we all said, "He had to be an angel!"

What a trip! That was a trip the four of us will never forget!

The Miracle

...in order to be a realist, you most believe in miracles.

—DAVID BEN-GURION

He heals the brokenhearted, and binds up their wounds.

—PSALM 147:3 (RSV)

PEOPLE SEEM TO THINK MIRACLES only happened a long time ago. Not true....miracles happen every day.

As I placed the telephone back in its cradle, I marveled at the story I had just heard. It isn't every day that one hears about a miracle, but when one does, it lifts the spirit and renews ones faith.

My editor had requested several extra angel stories for my book. I had put out a call to my friend Sara O'Meara and she had returned my call immediately. She offered to send me several in which she had been involved. Then she generously told me about her blessed healing.

It was twenty-five years ago when Sara was told that her body was riddled with cancer. She had five doctors who told her that the cancer had spread to every gland in her body. They all agreed that she wouldn't make it, that she had less than three months to live.

Sara said, "You can't imagine how I felt when I was told that my life was going to be snuffed out so soon. At that time I had two little boys to raise all by myself, so that was quite a blow!"

Sara remained in the hospital until something happened that would change her life forever. She told me that she was in her hospital room with the television on when an advertisement came on for the noted healer Kathryn[1] Kuhlman's upcoming appearance in the area.

Sara said, "She was talking to me, you know. I mean right to me, because Kathryn Kuhlman said, 'Be at the Shrine Auditorium in Los Angeles this Sunday, because you need a miracle!'

"I thought, I'm going to be there."

Sara told me she was brought up Presbyterian, and in fact she and her best friend Yvonne had met as Presbyterian Sunday school teachers. Sara admitted, "We never really knew about healings, I mean the healing services. After all, they seemed like the 'Holy Roller' types, where people make all that noise. But I decided I didn't care. I didn't care what it was. I was going to be there...and there I was."

But it took some doing. Sara wasn't supposed to be out of the hospital until four days after the Sunday that Kathryn Kuhlman was appearing at the Shrine Auditorium in Los Angeles. Sara insisted on getting out of the hospital before that Sunday. "I knew I was going to be there...that I had to be there."

When Sara left the hospital she was very weak. She had an incision on one side of her body that was eighteen inches long. That was before they had stitches that dissolved, so Sara had clamps. Because of the extensive surgery, the doctor told her that she would have to go home, stay in bed and not move around. Otherwise she couldn't go home. Sara promised.

1Kathryn Kuhlman; Born 5/9/07-Died 2/20/76. Famous Amer. Evangelist and faith healer.

Someone once said promises are made to be broken. Sara had an appointment with destiny, and nothing was going to stop her.

When Sunday arrived, Yvonne picked Sara up in her car and drove her to the Shrine Auditorium. She was in pain and discomfort, but she insisted on going to see Kathryn Kuhlman regardless of how she felt.

By the time Sara had walked all the way from the car and into the auditorium, she was bleeding profusely and she was becoming extremely weak. Her friend asked her, "Do you think you're going to make it?"

Sara told her, "I have to be inside."

But when Sara walked up to the entrance, the doors were closed. The ushers said every chair had been taken, and they could not let her in.

Sara was absolutely floored! She couldn't believe it.

Just then the door opened and a woman came outside. It was another friend of Sara's. It seems she had come outside to get a sweater from her car because it was cold in the auditorium. With surprise she asked, "What in the world are you doing here, Sara?"

Sara told her, "I'm not feeling well, and I had hoped to get in, but there are no seats left."

Her friend immediately responded with, "You take my seat, and my husband will give his seat to your friend."

Usually Sara would have said, "No, no, no," but instead she said, "I'd love to."

The seats were at the top of the first balcony in the last row. By the time Sara had climbed the steps she was completely exhausted.

Sara told me at that point that she didn't know what Kathryn Kuhlman was saying up on the stage. She said, "It was as if I was being lifted up and I knew that either I was dying, hallucinating or something fabulous was happening to me, and I wasn't sure what."

Kathryn Kuhlman was speaking when suddenly she stopped and said, "There's a wonderful healing of cancer up there in the balcony. It's a girl who has cancer throughout her body."

Sara said, "I knew at once that something wonderful was happening and I was absolutely thrilled. Perhaps it was me, and so I prayed. I said, 'God, if You are touching me, please let me know it in a very real way.'"

Kathryn continued to talk and all of a sudden she stopped again, and said, "The girl will know it! It's like a thousand needles going through her body all at one time."

Sara continued, "It was true! It was as if I had a hold of an electrical current. A thousand volts of electricity! I knew then that something *wonderful* was happening to me."

Unbeknownst to Sara at the time, the entire row of people sitting next to her had been knocked down from the surge of power. They couldn't even sit up. Sara was later told about it by Sister Mary Ignacius, who was sitting in the same row.

Kathryn Kuhlman continued talking, then she stopped again and said, "The girl sitting in the last row of the first balcony in a red dress. "Stand up," she commanded. "You are healed!"

Sara said, "I knew she was talking to me, but I couldn't stand up because I was shaking so hard."

The ushers went up to Sara and said, "Aren't you the one that's been healed?" Sara answered, "Yes."

Then they said, "Well, go down and give your testimony."

Sara paused. She didn't know if she could do that. She thought, *Go down in front of all these people and tell them what has happened to me, something so personal?*

Then it was as if a voice said, "You mean, I would do this for you, and you would not give Me the glory?"

Sara said, "I tell you, that voice was strong inside me!"

She got up, and as she did, the energy soared throughout her body. She felt like a different human being. The bleeding had stopped. She raced, literally raced down the steps.

As she walked down the aisle on the main floor to get to Kathryn, she saw other people who had also been healed, and they were most anxious to get up on the stage. Sara thought, *Oh good, she'll never reach me because they want to go and I'll just kind of meander on down.*

Kathryn called to her and said, "You in the red dress, get up here, the Glory of God is all over you!" She was very dramatic. She went on, "Get up here and tell what God has done for you, for He has saved you for a very special purpose."

Sara got up onstage and revealed what had happened to her. "I told about the fact that while I was sitting there, I saw a pink cloud come from the right side of the auditorium. It came floating toward me and surrounded me. I have never seen it since. I told every detail of the story and the people were very quiet. They knew it had really happened."

Sara was supposed to go back to the doctor on Monday morning and she did. Her dear friend Yvonne took her and sat in the waiting room while Sara was in with the doctor. Sara hadn't been in the examining room very long when the doctor came flying out of the room and said to Yvonne, "You have the craziest friend I've ever seen. She has completely healed! There's nothing there!"

Sara went on to explain, "After he had examined me, I was able to tell him about the miracle. He's never been the same since, nor have I."

She added, "It was a very special date when I was healed, not only because God had given me a second chance in life, but because my older son had been born on the same date, February 20. It was also the date that Kathryn Kuhlman would be taken home to God years later."

Sara O'Meara worked with Kathryn Kuhlman until Kathryn's death. Sara is co-founder of Childhelp, an organization dedicated to helping children.

She is living proof that miracles do happen.

The Face of God

Those who possess insight…talk to the angels and learn many things from them.
The suggestion and revelation that the angels communicate,
is according to the nature of the person concerned.

—MIRZA GHULAM AHMAD

And his face was like the sun shining in full strength.

—REVELATION 1:16 (RSV)

INA B. LIVES IN CALIFORNIA with her husband and two-year-old child. A natural intuitive and a definite believer in angels, she works two days a week counseling people with their problems.

When I was three and a half years old, my sister and I moved into a new house with my mother and her new husband. My mother had just remarried, and being a small child with a new stepfather, there were a lot of adjustments to be made. For whatever reasons, the move to the new house was not easy. From the time we moved into the new house, I had a feeling of something different. There was something about the house that made me feel uncomfortable and alone.

It was during this time, when I was reaching out for someone, yearning for something or someone to give me comfort, that my story begins.

It was about three months after we had moved into our new house when something unusual started to occur. The first time it happened, I had gone to bed and just as I was drifting off to sleep, I felt someone caressing my cheek and my hair ever so gently. It was such a loving caress, like the down of a feather against my cheek or an angel's kiss. It felt wonderful. Then to my delight the fragrance of flowers like lilacs filled my rooms.

When I reached out to touch the person who was caressing my cheek, there was no one there! I couldn't feel anyone! I opened my eyes and there was no one in my room—but I could still smell the flowers. The scent of the flowers made me feel safe and secure, and I drifted off to sleep, feeling as if someone was with me.

The gentle caresses and the fragrance of the flowers continued every night for several weeks, and I went from a feeling of being lonely to a feeling of well-being.

One night when I awoke to the scent of flowers, I went into my mother's room and told her all about the invisible visitor and the wonderful smell of flowers. Considering how strange my story must have sounded, she and my stepfather were very understanding. They took me back to my room, tucked me in and sat on the bed with me. They thought I must have been dreaming, but I knew I wasn't.

A few nights later I awoke just before dawn. My room looked different, as if there was a golden mist in my room. I don't know how else to describe it, just an entire room filled with a sparkling golden mist.

My bed was next to the window, so when I looked outside I could see the sunrise. Something told me to look at the clouds in the predawn light, and when I did, I saw…Jesus' face! Everything was pastel and so soft. His hair, His features, everything about Him emanated love. He was absolutely beautiful! I remember feeling drawn to Him and I literally left my body, left my room and went toward Him as He held out His hands to me.

Somehow He communicated with me, telling me, "I am you and you are Me, we're all the same."

Then He embraced me, enfolding me gently with His arms and His love. I was conscious of being in the air and having the most loving, joyous feeling I have ever known to this day.

He then said, "Everything continues. There is no time. There is no death. There is a true connection to everything….The Bible is not all there is."

I remember being told, "There are other ways to get there [to heaven]. There are many nice ways."

He told me many things.

He also told me that my family and I would always be protected no matter what happened.

When I was back in my bed, I thought, "I have to tell Mom I died and came back."

That's what I thought had happened to me. After all, I was barely four years old.

When I told Mom about the "wonderful thing" that had happened to me, she told me, "There's no way it could have really happened."

She kept talking to me, telling me, "You just had a dream. Things like what you are talking about just don't happen."

Finally, I believed her.

But whatever had happened to me changed my life forever.

It gave me a self-confidence I'd never had. I felt safe and secure and I have continued to feel so ever since that morning. I believed in the "God Face." That is what I came to call the loving face I saw when I was a little girl.

Whenever I have a problem or need help, I see the God Face in my mind and I pray to him.

He has always answered my prayers.

Many years later, we were still living in California. I was twenty-three years old and working as the manager of a cute, quaint, metaphysical bookstore in an L-shaped shopping center. Since I was the manager, I worked at night so I could lock up the store and make the night deposit. We usually had fifteen hundred dollars each day, and I always took care of the money myself.

For about a week I had been feeling uneasy at work. In fact, I had even called two of my male friends and asked them to come by work when I was closing so that I would have someone with me when I dropped the money at the night deposit.

We always had a lot of customers, or visitors as we liked to call them, in the evening, and this evening was no different from any other. A good friend of mine, Jane, had stopped by and we were going to go out for coffee and a chat after I got off work. The evening seemed to be progressing normally when the front door suddenly burst open and a man wearing a full-face ski mask sauntered into the store with a revolver in his hand and a very cocky attitude.

I was standing in front of the counter near the cash register when he pointed his gun at me and, motioning with his head and hands, demanded, "Give me the money!"

I was in no position to argue, and not wanting anyone to be hurt, I emptied the tray out of the cash register. Without his telling me to, I turned and went right over to the other cash register, took out the entire tray and handed him both of them. All the time I was thinking, *Stay calm, stay calm, don't lose control.*

Taking both trays, he then turned on me as if to say, *I'm not done yet.* Out of that entire room, he seemed to know that Jane was my girlfriend. Jane was crying at this point, and motioning to her, he grabbed her and made her stand next to me.

I didn't know what to expect next, but I kept thinking, *I have to be calm no matter what happens.*

Then he put the gun to my forehead and looked at my friend, still silent but seeming to ask her, *Should I shoot her in the head? Or should I shoot her in the heart?* As he dug the nozzle of the gun into my chest, I thought I was going to die.

My friend Jane was crying hysterically.

All I could think was, *Oh God, they're going to have to call my mom and tell her I've been murdered, that I'm dead.*

Then in fear and desperation, I did what I've always done in times of need: I silently prayed to my angel, to the God Face.

Help me, God. Help Jane. Oh please, help all of us. Please save our lives. Save us from this maniac.

Then I heard a voice say, "You're safe."

While I continued to pray, the robber suddenly bolted and ran out of the shop as if he had seen a ghost! He didn't back up holding the gun on us as he left. He acted as if he had seen or heard something that had scared him out of his wits, and he ran for his life!

We all looked at one another, absolutely stunned!

To say we were badly shaken from what had just taken place would be an understatement. My legs were shaking so badly I didn't think I could walk.

What really seemed peculiar was the way the robber had suddenly bolted out of the store, as if a team of wild horses were after him. We didn't know why he had left so suddenly—but were we ever thankful he had!

Now that isn't the end of the story.

After our horrendous experience, I continued to pray every day that the robber would be caught and the money returned. One week later to the day, the robber was picked up and arrested in Oregon, trying to cash my personal check, a check that I had put in the cash register the day of the robbery.

All my prayers were answered and in a way I could never imagine.

Generosity and Blessings
(The Man in Black)

There's no such thing as an unimportant act of kindness.
—ANONYMOUS

*Give, and it will be given unto you; good measure, pressed down,
shaken together, running over, will be put into your lap.*
—LUKE 6:38 (RSV)

CYNTHIA LACHANCE HAS HAD a number of angelic encounters.

Times had been very difficult for us financially the year this unusual incident took place. We had been selling Indian jewelry for several years, but in 1979 the jewelry market had really slowed down. We also had some personal setbacks that contributed to our financial problems. What I am about to tell you took place in California in a small town just outside of Riverside.

It was Friday evening, and I had gone over to the local laundromat to do our laundry while my husband stayed back at the motel and sorted out the jewelry we would be selling at the local swap meet the next day. We had been in

California going on three weeks, and the turnout at the swap meet on Saturdays and Sundays wasn't at all what we had expected. We had hoped for much better sales and were disappointed with the results of our efforts. To top things off, now it looked as if the weather was going to be rainy all weekend. We considered not going to the swap meet at all, but finally decided to give it one last try. We were so broke we really didn't have much choice. As a matter of fact, I had to go through our pockets and the bottom of my purse to find what I thought would be enough change to do the laundry.

When I entered the laundromat it was practically empty. I was almost through doing the laundry when a man dressed in dark clothing came up to me. I felt a little uneasy, perhaps because I didn't know what he wanted, and also because of his black attire.

Then he spoke. "Excuse me, ma'am, do you have any change? Say a quarter for a cup of coffee?"

All the money I had left was the little bit of change I had in my pocket. It couldn't have amounted to a dollar in all. Being well versed in the Bible, I thought, "If you do it unto the least of these, you do it unto me."

This stranger had asked for help and I had to help him if I could. I looked at the man, smiled and, taking what was left of the change I had in my pocket, I gave it to him. Every cent I had.

As he took the change, he nodded his head and said, "Thank you, ma'am."

I glanced over at the dryer for a moment and turned back to look at the stranger, and he was gone! I mean disappeared! It was as if he had gone up in a puff of smoke. I looked around the laundromat and he was nowhere in sight. I even went to the front door and looked around outside. I knew that I wouldn't find him.

When I returned to the motel where we were staying, I neglected to tell my husband about the man in black and the fact that I had given our last cent to a stranger. I didn't feel like a lecture before going to bed.

When we arrived at the swap meet the next day, the sky was overcast and threatening rain. We stood there and wondered if we should set up our display or head back to Arizona and home. Something told me we should give it a try, so we proceeded to open up shop and wait for the bargain hunters to arrive.

There seemed to be a steady flow of traffic all day, no more and no less than there had been on the last two weekends. The day passed slowly. I even had time for lunch. By the end of the day we were both tired and hungry, but we decided to go back to our room before getting something to eat.

On our way back my husband said optimistically, "I think we did pretty good today, but we'll count our money later."

Can you imagine our surprise, when, after dinner, we counted our earnings for the day and discovered we had made more than double what we normally make? As a matter of fact, it was the most we had ever made in one day!

Coincidence? I don't think so.

I believe we had help from a very special stranger...*the man in black*...an angel who asked for a quarter to buy a cup of coffee.

Saved by Angels

THIS EXTRAORDINARY STORY was told to me by Margaret Kroeger, a truly remarkable woman who died in 1996. It is included as a tribute to Margaret and her belief in everyday miracles.

It was one of those beautiful spring days that makes a person glad to be alive. Margaret had been in Fort Lauderdale going on appointments all day. Finally finished, she was on her way to the parking lot to pick up her car. She was looking forward to getting home and going for a swim in the pool where she lived.

As she stood at the corner of the intersection with the warm sun on her back, waiting for the light to turn green, she mentally repeated an affirmation prayer of divine protection. Margaret strongly believed in the power of prayer and she used it daily, not just in times of crisis as so many of us do.

The sign turned green, and as Margaret stepped off the curb, her vision was suddenly obstructed by a cascade of white and golden sparkling stars shooting across in front of her eyes. She was so startled, that she stepped backward, back onto the curb.

She described the incident as being somewhat similar to bending over and standing up too fast, and then seeing a few stars. "At first," she said, "There were so many, they were so thick, that I couldn't see to walk across the street. They were absolutely beautiful, but at the time I wondered where they came from. The shower of sparkling stars gradually dissipated, and just as I was about to start across the street again, a speeding car careened around the corner and smashed into the cars that were waiting for the signal to change! A piece of metal hit me in the arm as it flew by me.

If I had been walking across the street, I would have been killed!"

The driver of the car was killed. Margaret said that she thought he was blinded by the sun, panicked and thus lost control of his car.

Whatever had happened, she believed that her life had been spared by angelic beings.

What happened to Margaret Kroeger was truly divine intervention, a power much greater than man and beyond mortal comprehension.

Margaret blessed all of us with her wit, intelligence and, above all, her spirituality for eight more years. She was a true and loyal friend.

In Loving Memory of Margaret Kroeger

"Big Red," Angel Dog

How much do you know that I've just begun to understand?
Spirit of grace and humor on all fours.
—PAM REINKE

I heard around the throne and the living creatures...the voice of many angels....
—REVELATION 5:11 (RSV)

HERE ARE MANY INSTANCES of animals rescuing people. This story confirms that it really does happen. Margaret Kroeger was living in Colorado when this incident occurred. It made an indelible impression on my daughter Debby as a teenager.

One evening in Minnesota, we were sitting around talking about unusual events that had taken place in our lives, when Margaret said she had a story she had never shared with anyone because she thought no one would believe her. She said she wanted to keep the memory of it because it was so precious to her. She evidently felt we would believe her, or at least have the courtesy not to make fun of her. So she started to tell us her story.

Margaret said she was traveling alone, driving back to Denver from Longmont, when she noticed a hitchhiker along the side of the road. He was a nice-looking young man, clean shaven, light brown hair, with a small traveling bag sitting on the ground. He certainly looked safe enough to pick up, and besides, she was tired of driving alone.

She stopped the car and backed up to pick up the hitchhiker. He smiled as she approached, and Margaret thought how nice it would be to have company the rest of the way home. She hoped he was a good conversationalist.

The second the young man opened the door, Margaret said, "I had a funny feeling that something wasn't right. I should have driven off right then and there. But I didn't listen to my intuition. Instead, I asked him his name and where he was going."

He smiled at her and in a most charming way, answered, "Oh, just up the road a piece. As far as you're going. Just call me Jim."

Again, she had that uneasy feeling.

"My name is Margaret and I'm going to Denver. Is that far enough for you?"

He smiled, "That's far enough." he said as he set his bag on the floor and sat down in the passenger seat next to her.

She had the radio playing and classical music floated through the air as she pulled back onto the highway. The next thing she knew he was adjusting the radio, hitting the buttons to change the stations. When he found some jazz he turned the volume up and started to tap his fingers against the dashboard, not saying a word.

She asked him to please turn the radio down, but either he was deaf or he was deliberately ignoring her, because he turned it up even louder than it was before. "That was when I knew I was in trouble!" said Margaret.

She knew she had made a mistake picking up a stranger but she had to concentrate on the road. She didn't want to do something stupid and end up having an accident. She thought, *I've picked up a jerk, I'd better make the best of the situation.* Then the man lit a cigarette.

"That did it! No one smokes in my car," Margaret told us. "I started to slow down and I pulled over to the side of the road to stop. As I did so, he pulled a knife on me!"

"Give me your purse!" he shouted, "Now!"

She was so stunned that for a moment she froze. She still had her foot on the brake and her hands were tightly gripping the steering wheel as she screeched to a halt. He had the knife pointed at her throat and she was afraid to move.

Suddenly, out of the backseat of the car she heard a low, deep growl, and out of the corner of her eye she caught the movement of red fur. Then she saw him.

"It was my old dog, Big Red, baring his teeth, ready to attack!"

Unexpectedly, the man pulled back the knife and grabbed the door handle. As he swung the door open, the big red Irish setter leaped over the seat and charged at the man with his teeth bared. The man half-fell, half-crawled out of the car onto the ground. As he climbed to his feet and tried to get away, the dog followed him in hot pursuit, alternately growling and then charging.

At this point Margaret's adrenaline was working overtime. She reached over and grabbed the door, slamming it shut. She watched as the big red dog chased that horrible man into the woods. Then she slammed the car into gear and started to take off.

"Then I thought of the dog," Margaret continued. "I don't know why, but I stopped the car. I looked back, but he was already out of sight. Besides, I knew I wouldn't see Red again. You see, Red, my dear friend, had been put to sleep two years ago. As unbelievable as it may seem, Red had appeared out of nowhere to protect me.

"What I truly believe is that it was an angel in the intimidating form of an angry dog that appeared to frighten off my attacker, but in a form I wouldn't be afraid of.

"By the time I got to Denver it was getting dark. I was just thankful to be home. If my guardian angel hadn't been working overtime, I probably wouldn't even be alive. As I pulled into my driveway, I said a prayer of thanksgiving...to Big Red for having been in my life, and to my Guardian Angel for protecting me."

Smoky Mountain Angels

Give me somewhere to stand, and I will move the earth.
—ARCHIMEDES

Who shall ascend the hill of the Lord? And who shall stand in his holy place?
—PSALM 24:3 (RSV)

A RIDE THAT IS UNEXPLAINABLE—unless you have faith. Gloria told us this story about her family trip that took place many years ago.

When we started out on the trip, my sister Carolyn didn't want to go with us, but Mother and Dad wouldn't let her stay home alone. Besides, she would have missed the experience of a lifetime: We were driving from Minnesota to Florida by car to visit Dad's lifelong friend Kenny, who was sick with cancer. My sister had been sitting in the back seat pouting ever since we left home, but I was glad to be going on the trip.

It was a beautiful sunny morning when we started to weave our way through the Great Smoky Mountains in Tennessee. There was a haze over the mountains and dew on the leaves from last night's rainfall. The scenery had almost an ethereal quality about it. It was beautiful.

We had eaten a delicious breakfast at the place where we had stayed, and for the first time since we had left home everyone seemed pretty contented. Music was playing on the radio and Mother was trying to figure out how to fold the map so she could put it away in the glove compartment. We were driving up the side of a mountain, and of all things we started to talk about how far down the mountain the drop was on the passenger side of the car.

Dad told us, "Look straight ahead, and then the drop won't bother you so much."

It was while we were talking about "what if this happened, or what if that happened" that a semitrailer rounded the side of the mountain and headed toward us on the other side of the road. It was only a two-lane road, but as long as the truck stayed on his own side of the road, everything would be okay.

Everything was going along just fine, when suddenly another huge semi with a heavy load came around the curve going too fast and pulled out into our lane to pass the other truck. He was coming down the mountain headed straight at us!!

We knew that we'd be pushed off the side of the mountain and killed if the semi hit us. What could we do? There was absolutely no place to go to get out of the way of the oncoming semitrailer.

It was at that moment that Dad spotted a little filling station jutting out the side of the mountain with a big U-shaped driveway. Mom had turned off the radio and no one said a word. Everyone was holding their breath and silently praying that we'd come out of the situation alive. It was almost as if we were suspended in time.

Instead of slowing down, Dad stepped on the accelerator as hard as he could, and headed up the mountain toward the semi at full speed! I couldn't believe it! You should have seen us. It looked as if we were trying to crash into each other!

Just when we were within a few feet of each other, and I thought we were going to crash for sure, Dad whipped the steering wheel around and we cut into the driveway of the filling station and out the other end of the driveway, barely missing the tailgate of the semi!

No one said a word. No one said a word for five minutes! We gradually let out a sigh of relief and slowly started to breathe normally again. We had been holding our breath during that entire hair-raising ride.

Dad said that when he looked in the rearview mirror to see if we were okay, my sister and I looked as if all the blood had been drained from our faces. We were white as a sheet. Believe me, after that experience you would have been, too.

Thankfully, the rest of the trip did not include any more hair-raising incidents. We decided that on our way home we would stop and visit with the people that ran the station and tell them what had happened to us. We wanted to let them know how their station had saved our lives.

We took the same route home, but look as we might, we couldn't find a station anywhere on the side of that mountain! We finally gave up looking for it.

When we got to the next small town, we stopped and asked if anyone knew where the station was on that road. The owner of the general store said, "There used to be a filling station up there, but it's been gone for years."

A ghost filling station? I don't think so. I think guardian angels put the station back in place to save my family. I believe the angels knew my dad had helped many people during the Great Depression with free gas when he owned a filling station, and they rewarded him by providing one for him to save his family.

Thanks to Dad's excellent driving, we all survived.

Years later, when we were talking about the trip to Florida, Dad said, "Don't say anything to the rest of the family, but it was as if someone else was driving the car that day.

"There was a power greater than mine in the car. Until now I've never told that to anyone."

"Keep the Faith"

Coincidence is God's way of performing miracles anonymously.
—SOPHY BURNHAM, Angel Letters, 1991

So we are always of good courage; ...we walk by faith, not by sight.
—II CORINTHIANS 5:6-7 (RSV)

❧

THIS STORY HAPPENED TO US not long ago. We believe the man who crossed my path was an angel in disguise.

My husband Les and I were at the Dallas-Fort Worth Airport waiting for our return flight to Arizona when I had a most unusual encounter.

Not knowing how long it would take to get to the airport, we had arrived early for our flight. There were only about a half dozen people wandering around the America West section of the terminal, so it was rather quiet. Les suggested we get a pizza for lunch—his favorite—which we did.

I was seated, enjoying my slice of pizza, when Les told me he would be back in a few minutes. He was going to the restroom to wash his hands. I watched as he slowly walked away, noting his limp from the auto accident two years earlier.

His health had been slowly failing ever since the accident, and I wondered if he would still be with me a year from now.

Les was about fifty feet from me when a tall, rather plump, pleasant-looking man dressed in khaki pants, a golf shirt and a cap with a bill walked up and stopped five feet in front of me. He looked at me, then he turned his head and looked at Les, then he turned back to me and said, "Absolutely" as if in answer to the silent question I had just asked.

I looked at the man, wondering if that was what he meant, and he repeated the same word twice: "Absolutely, absolutely." He did seem to be answering my questioning thoughts.

I wiped my lips and said, "That's my husband."

He responded with, "I know."

Then he turned as if he was going to continue on his way, but then he paused. He turned and looked at me again, and softly said, "Keep the faith."

I smiled at him and replied, "Thank you, I will."

He had the most loving expression on his face when he looked at me. In fact, his entire presence was gentle and loving.

Then again he said, "Don't lose faith."

As he started to turn away, he paused and repeated the phrase for a third and final time saying, "Remember to keep the faith."

With that, still smiling, he turned and slowly walked away.

Puzzled, I watched as the stranger walked down the corridor. He never stopped, nor did I see him speak to another person. Eventually he disappeared from my sight—but not from my mind.

When we arrived home, I called my daughter and son-in-law to let them know we had arrived home safely. Our family has always done that. I also told them about the stranger I had met at the airport terminal and the short, strange conversation I had with him. My son-in-law commented, "Katheryn, your mother has the strangest things happen to her."

But my daughter said, "Mother, perhaps he was an angel."

Who was the kindly man who spoke to me at the terminal? What did he mean, "absolutely"?

Whoever he was, his message of faith has helped sustain me during some very difficult times. In the next eight months I buried both my mother and father, as well as a dear friend of thirty years.

Les, who has chronic obstructive pulmonary lung disease, COPD, is still with me. He has managed to control his illness with medication. It has been over a year since the stranger spoke to me. He was "absolutely" correct about my husband.

Was the stranger an angel in disguise, telling me to hold on? Perhaps. I would like to think so. Or was he a well-meaning stranger? Whoever he was, his loving message was certainly most appropriate and reinforces the belief that we must..."Keep the faith."

The Angel of Healing

MIRACLES HAPPEN EVERY DAY—we just have to open our eyes so we can see them.

It has been almost thirty years since we witnessed the miracle that took place at the Shrine Auditorium in Minneapolis, Minnesota, on a warm Sunday afternoon.

My husband Les and I were attending a healing service being held by Katheryn Kuhlman in the hopes that my husband would be healed of asthma. The auditorium was filled to overflowing, with the wheelchair section in the center of the ground floor. We were up in the center of the second balcony almost in the last row. Several of our friends were nearby, including Bob and Bev Moring and one of the ministers from a local church with his son, who was in a back brace. They all witnessed what happened during the service that wonderful Sunday.

Katheryn Kuhlman was on the stage praying, holding her arms out over her head toward the crowd of people in the packed auditorium. We were about twenty minutes into the service when a commotion started several rows in front of us. At first we didn't think anything about it until we heard someone say, "He's been healed!"

There were so many people around us that we didn't know who had been healed or exactly what they were talking about. The commotion continued until ushers came down the steps and reached into the row where the minister was sitting and took his son's hand and helped him out to the aisle. It seemed that it was the minister's son who had been healed!

The ushers then helped the young man finish taking off what appeared to be some kind of thick, brown leather vest with heavy buckles. The young man held it up in the air and, with a look of amazement on his face, walked erect with the ushers to the exit.

Everyone was crying and shouting, "Praise the Lord" and "Thank you, dear Jesus." It was sheer pandemonium. We looked on, not fully comprehending what kind of a healing had just taken place. We believed the young man had been healed, but from what? We waited expectantly to see what would happen next.

On the main floor, people were going up onstage to tell of their healings, but we were anxiously waiting for the twelve-year-old boy to appear. It was hard to find him in such a crowd of people.

When he finally got to the stage, he walked right up the steps, waving the brace in the air over his head as he stood perfectly straight!

Katheryn Kuhlman asked him some questions. He told her that he had been in the back brace to try to help straighten his spine for the last four years. He had been so crippled, so bent over before the healing, that he could hardly hold his head up to look straight ahead.

The boy said, "When you started to pray, I listened to every word you said, and I asked Jesus to heal me.

It was when I was praying, my back started to make funny, cracking sounds. I felt warm and tingling all over. I could feel my back trying to push out of the brace. The people in the row behind me said they could hear my back cracking. I asked someone to help me unbuckle the back of the brace, and they did."

He said simply, "It doesn't hurt anymore. I think I've been healed."

The following week the minister from Bob and Bev's church went to the home of the young man to see how the family was doing since their son had been healed, and of course to see how the young man was getting along. It is interesting to note that the young man is doing extremely well.

As for the family, they have been having a little trouble adjusting to the healthy young man they now have living with them.

The doctors still can't believe it and, from what I last heard, were running innumerable tests.

World War II Angel

*Lead them straight and true; give strength to their arms, stoutness to their
hearts, steadfastness in their faith....*

—FRANKLIN D. ROOSEVELT, JUNE 6, 1944

Though war arise against me, yet I will be confident.

—PSALM 27:3 (RSV)

OBERT J. BUCKLEY, FORMER CEO of Allegheny International,
recounted this tale from his experiences in battle when he was
nineteen years old.

The 75th Division of the First Army, to which I belonged, was
being called back into action. We were going to go back to the front line in a
counteroffensive to the Battle of the Bulge. We had just finished having a few
days of R and R (rest and recuperation), in Liege, Belgium, so we felt pretty
good. Just before we left for the front, we had mail call and I was fortunate to
receive some mail from home. Among my mail was a letter from my mother,
which was really nice because she didn't write too often.

As we boarded the transport truck, I thought about what Mom had said in
her letter. She had closed with the prayer, "I pray that the Virgin Mary will

throw her cloak around you to cover you and protect you in battle." I thought how lucky I was to have a mother who loved me so much and prayed for me. But then, she loved all three of her children. She was a very special lady.

There were thirteen of us in the back of the truck as we drove toward our destination. It was on the outskirts of a town, that the shelling started. The Germans were shooting their basic 88mm artillery shells as we were trying to move out. They were pretty darned accurate with them.

Then we were hit! It was in the right front wheel. The explosion was horrific. Shrapnel was flying everywhere and bits and pieces of metal from both the shell and the truck filled the air. It's truly amazing that the entire truck wasn't blown up—they usually were. A two-and-a-half-ton truck is nothing against an 88mm shell.

During the explosion I was knocked unconscious, but I don't think for long. When I came to, I felt as if I was wrapped in velvet. When I tried to get up, I discovered that I was entangled in the canvas that had been covering the top of the truck. Somewhat puzzled, I looked at it, wondering why it had felt like velvet to me.

When I looked around me and saw the devastation, I realized how lucky I was to be alive. I must have had a guardian angel on my shoulder, for to survive without a scratch was like a miracle. Of the thirteen men that were riding in the back of the truck with me, six were killed instantly and five were severely injured. One of the men had his right kidney hanging out of his back. Three of the five that were injured survived.

Then I saw him—Dr. Schwartz, from St. Louis, Missouri. He moved among the injured and dying, administering medical aid as if he was protected from all harm. He had absolutely no fear for his own life! Shells were still coming in but he seemed oblivious to them. His only concern was for the injured men whose lives he was trying to save. I tried to help him by moving some of the bodies out of the way and the injured to safety. I did whatever he asked me to do. I'll never forget him…he was the bravest man I've ever known.

When the wounded had been taken away, the rest of us walked on, out of the line of fire. As I did so, I looked up and saw one man besides myself that had survived the blast. His name was Louis Dotson, from Chattanooga, Tennessee. I'll never forget the way he jumped down from the wreckage at the back of the truck, smiled and said, "Well, it's a nice day for a walk anyway."

When he said that, I laughed, then we both laughed. We were relieved just to be alive. He was a great guy.

I believe that I was saved that day by my mother's prayers, and that I was blessed to see the epitome of an angel in Dr. Schwartz.

Two blessings in one day are more than any man could ever ask for.

Angelic Aid

PAT ELWOOD'S NIECE, GERI KEMP-COLE, was saved from death by an angel. This remarkable story took place in Southern California.

It was Friday the thirteenth, December 1996, and nothing out of the ordinary had happened that day, Geri thought, as she tucked her five-year-old daughter Krystal into bed and kissed her good night. Besides, she wasn't superstitious. Her husband Tom worked out of town on Friday nights. So, as a treat, Krystal got to sleep with her mother in the king-sized bed in the master bedroom when her daddy was gone.

Geri felt exhausted after a very busy day, so she decided to retire early. As she secured the house, set the burglar alarm and put their two dogs outside, she looked forward to getting a good night's sleep.

Once upstairs, she followed her usual routine of closing the doors to the bedroom to keep the warmth from the fireplace in the high ceilinged room.

There was a smoke detector in the hallway and before getting into bed, Geri checked the fire, making sure the drawstring screen was pulled securely across the fireplace opening. Finally, after finishing her routine, she was able to fall into bed and was soon sound asleep beside her young daughter.

Two hours later, around eleven, Geri was abruptly awakened by a hand shaking her right shoulder and arm, and a voice urgently saying, "Wake up! Wake up! Look over there!"

Geri bolted upright in bed and to her horror saw that the whole room was aglow! Her bed was covered with ashes! The carpet was burning, the upholstered chair was ablaze and the entire wall next to the fireplace had caught on fire from sparks that were coming from a bucket of burning kindling wood nearby. The glow from the quickly moving fire lit the room, and heavy black smoke curled two or three feet from the ceiling, moving lower and closer with every second.

Leaping out of bed, Geri grabbed her still sleeping daughter and ran out of the room, down the stairs and with her adrenaline pumping full force made it safely outside of the house within seconds. She later said she had never moved that fast in her entire life!

She quickly placed a bewildered and now wide awake Krystal in her car, telling her to "Stay there!"

When Geri had opened the outside door, she had set off the burglar alarm and their telephone automatically called the alarm company. Geri returned to the house and tried to dial the fire department, but with the alarm system in use, she couldn't get through because her line was busy. She grabbed an outside garden hose located near the doorway and, turning it on full force, breathed a prayer of thanks that it hadn't frozen that cold night. Slipping and sliding on her now wet marble floor in the entry, she somehow managed to pull the hose into the house and up the stairs.

As she tried to enter her bedroom, the smoke was so thick that all she could see was the glow from the fire. Geri dropped to her hands and knees and, shielding her nose and mouth, she beseeched God to help her as she crawled close enough to spray the flames that were trying to devour her home. With great effort and determination she managed to get most of the fire out.

Geri went back downstairs, and her next attempt to call the fire department was successful. At the same time she called her neighbor, a quarter of a mile away, and they said they would be right over to help. She then had to run down to the bottom of their steep hill to unlock the iron gate that protected their property thus enabling the fire trucks to come in when they arrived.

Their neighbor arrived within minutes and helped Geri contain the rest of the fire. The fire department arrived forty minutes later, due to the distance they had to travel. The firefighters chopped through the bedroom wall to make sure the fire wasn't smoldering inside the wall. Firefighters believed that sparks popped out through a small gap in the middle of the fireplace screen, thus starting the fire on the rug that quickly spread.

Geri was transported to the emergency room in Murrieta to be treated for smoke inhalation. No one could believe how "lucky" Geri and Krystal were.

Geri doesn't believe that "luck" had anything to do with it! She hasn't a doubt in the world that it was her guardian angel who awakened her that awful night. Both she and Krystal were wearing their blessed brown scapular cloth medals, as they always did. Geri believes that the Blessed Mother sent "*angelic aid*" to save them from the devastating smoke and flames.

The new bedroom smoke detector that had been stored beneath their bed that night has now been installed in its proper place on the wall inside the bedroom. They no longer use their bedroom fireplace.

Geri's intelligent, cool thinking and physical agility come from years of being an avid, award-winning surfer, and also from having a private pilot's license. She worked for several years in the aviation industry, where keeping one's head is tantamount to survival.

Today Geri is the Assistant Supervisor of Business Support Services for the Temecula Valley Unified School District. She and her family still live in the home they built seven years ago in the rural hills above Murrieta, California, with their dogs and horses, and where this story took place.

Grandpa's Last Visit

Our life is an opening through which angels appear.
—ANONYMOUS

The angels will come out....
—MATTHEW 13:49 (RSV)

ICK CHURCHILL WAS FIRST and foremost a loving and devoted father and grandfather. He lived for his family and his love of flying.

Kim's father-in-law died the day before the following incident took place. In recounting what happened, she is as sure today as she was then that her father-in-law returned to see his grandsons one last time.

The boys—Hunter, age three, Collin, five and Cody, eight—were already asleep when Kim went in to check on her sons before getting herself ready for bed. Everyone was already sleeping. It had been a long day. As she brushed her teeth and put on her pajamas, she thought about how much they would all miss Dick. Just as she was going to lie down she heard a whirring and a clicking sound. At first she couldn't tell where it was coming from. She thought it was coming from the bathroom, but when she checked, the room was empty. She then stepped out into the hallway to listen, and she realized the sound was coming from her sons' room, which was right next door to her bedroom.

As she entered their room in the semidarkness she could see each of them in their beds sound asleep. They looked as if they hadn't moved since she had tucked them in. She could also hear the sound more clearly now, but what was it? She walked around the room looking at their things, trying to find whatever was making that strange noise. As she glanced at the bookcase, she spotted something—there it was! One of their race cars was sitting on the bookshelf, hung up on another toy, with its back wheels spinning. How strange...when she had been in the room only minutes earlier it certainly wasn't making any noise.

Looking around the room, Kim picked up the car and turned off the switch. As she put it back on the shelf, she felt that her father-in-law had been there. Without hesitation she went back to the bedroom and told her husband Dale, who was half asleep.

"Your dad was here. Believe it or not, he was here! He was in the boys' room."

Of course, Dale didn't believe her. At first, anyway.

The following morning Hunter didn't get up as he usually did. Normally he was the first one up and all over the place with boundless energy. Kim had to go into the bedroom to see what he was doing. She was surprised to find him still in bed, so she told him it was time for breakfast.

As he sat up he looked at her and asked, "Mom, will Grandpa be here for breakfast?"

Kim answered, "Don't you remember, Hunter? Grandpa died two days ago."

Hunter, in a very matter of fact tone, stated, "Grandpa was here last night."

She went on to explain everything all over again just to be sure he understood, but Hunter thought he had seen his grandpa the night before. Children often see things that adults don't. However, after listening to Hunter, Kim believed more firmly than ever that Dick had been there, in the boys' room, the night before.

Three hundred people attended the memorial service for Dick Churchill at the Champlain Airfighter Museum to pay tribute to this wonderful man's life. During the service the minister mentioned that Dick had returned to visit his grandchildren just the night before, letting them know that we live on after death.

Along with Dick's family and friends, his "Confederate Airforce Buddies" were there to pay homage to one of their fellow pilots. Kim said that as she looked around, she realized how fortunate they were to have known Dick and that he had played such an important part in their lives.

She said, "We'll never forget him."

An Angel's Warning

Angels offer their wings without being called upon.
—Creative Horizons

A word fitly spoken is like apples of gold in a setting of silver.
—Proverbs 25:11

THIS STORY BY ROBERT J. BUCKLEY, former CEO of Allegheny International, tells how he was angelically warned, thus saving his life.

It was an ordinary workday, but Bob was running late. At the last minute he decided to take the shortcut from his home on a seldom used, rustic, beat up old road through the woods from Sewickley into Pittsburgh. He hoped to make up time, but instead ended up having an experience he would never forget.

As he drove through the woods, he was mentally planning his schedule for the day. Revisions he would have to make were going through his head when he felt what he thought was a flat tire. It must have been that last bump he had hit. *Just what I need*, he thought, *I'm already late*. As he stopped the car and got out, he hoped there was a good spare in the trunk just in case he needed it.

He bent over to check the tire and as he did so, he heard a warning voice in his ear saying, "Watch out! Watch out behind you!"

Turning around he saw a mad, vicious Doberman pinscher about two hundred yards away from him racing down the road, legs flying. Bob was so taken off guard that at first he didn't realize that the dog was charging right at him! When he did realize it, he knew there wasn't enough time to get back into the car. Hoping to protect himself against the oncoming assault, Bob quickly crouched and braced himself against the car.

Within seconds the dog attacked! Leaning back on the car, Bob lifted both his feet off the ground and using them as weapons, kicked the Doberman in the chest with every ounce of strength he had, deflecting him into the air. The impact was so great that he could hear the dog's ribs cracking and see his eyes pop out of his head. The momentum sent the dog flying over Bob's head.

Severely shaken, Bob somehow managed to get to his feet. He stood there trembling and in shock. As he looked over at the dog, he knew the animal was dead.

It was at this point that the owner of the dog came running down the road. He had been chasing after the crazed dog trying to catch him. When he saw what had happened he asked Bob if he was hurt. Even though he was still shaky, Bob managed to tell the man that he would be okay in a few minutes. The owner of the dog went on to say that the dog had been acting funny lately. He said that while he was trying to take him to the veterinarian that morning to see what was wrong with him, the dog had broken loose and run into the woods. He had been chasing him ever since.

Again, the man wanted to know if Bob was all right, and he continued to apologize profusely. He was genuinely sorry for what had happened and was greatly relieved that Bob hadn't been physically hurt.

Finally, after regaining his composure, Bob started the car and headed into work. He knew that if it hadn't been for his training in the army he would never have known how to defend himself against such an attack. But most importantly, if he hadn't heard the warning voice, he would never have been able to turn around in time to defend himself.

Bob had horrible, terrifying dreams of the attack for many years. He still dreams about it once in a while. He believes that the voice he heard that morning was that of his guardian angel. If that Doberman had attacked him from behind without any warning, he surely would have been killed.

What Lies Beyond

IF THERE WAS ONLY ONE GIFT that I could give you, it would be for you to share my experience. Believe me when I tell you that it's much nicer on the other side. I know, because I've been there.

It was a blustery winter day in January 1971. The streets were icy, there was snow on the ground and the temperature hung around the twenty-degree mark. All I could hear was the siren blaring as the ambulance careened out of the main entrance of the St. Louis Park Medical Center headed for the hospital. The ambulance skidded and swayed as the nurse who was holding a bottle of plasma up over my head tried to maintain her balance. I tried the best I could to hold my arm straight for the transfusion that had been started to save my life. Now that I was on my way to the hospital, I realized just how lucky I was. If it hadn't been for Dr. Barno's critically decisive action, I wouldn't be here to tell you this story.

This was the day our daughter Debby was returning home from Panama with our granddaughter. She had been living there with her husband, who was in the Navy. We had planned to meet them at the airport at two o'clock. But life has a way of changing things: Just when we think we have everything under control, something unexpected always seems to happen.

When I awoke that morning, I had a stomachache and felt light-headed and weak. As the morning progressed, I continued to feel worse until my legs were so wobbly, I could hardly walk. When it was time for us to leave for the airport, I knew I was too weak to go. My daughter Katheryn, who had just come home from school, took one look at me and said, "We need to get Mom to a doctor— she's turning blue." Not realizing how sick I was, I told them first to go to the airport to pick up Debby, and then they could take me to the doctor. Katheryn wouldn't hear of it. If she had not insisted, I would have been dead by the time they returned home from the airport.

My husband and daughter drove me to the St. Louis Park Medical Center where I was helped into an examining room. When Dr. Barno opened the examining room door and saw me on the table, he yanked the door open wide and started yelling, "Plasma, plasma, quick! Get me some plasma!" Then he grabbed a scissors from the drawer and said he was going to cut off my sweater. I told him it was a brand-new sweater and I insisted on taking it off. Then I passed out. The next thing I knew I was being carried to the ambulance.

As the ambulance sped down Excelsior Boulevard on its way to the hospital, I closed my eyes and started to pray: "Dear God, If it's my time to go, please let me go quickly. If not, please help me." When I opened my eyes we had arrived at the hospital.

Within minutes I was rolled into the trauma unit where a highly efficient team of nurses and residents wrapped my arms and legs in an effort to try to compress my blood pressure. I remember looking at the nurse on my left, who was watching my blood pressure, and telling her, "I'm going to make it." She looked so worried that I felt as if I should try to reassure her. Then I said, "Take my watch and wedding ring and keep them for me until after surgery. I'll get them from you later."

The same nurse looked at Dr. Barno and with her voice rising said, "Her blood pressure is sixty over forty." I was bleeding internally and I was dying.

Then I heard bells ringing. They made a tinkling sound. They reminded me of something, but I couldn't remember what. I remember wondering why they had bells in the operating room. The next thing I knew, I had slipped out of my body and I was up in the corner of the room looking down at my body!

Everyone was frantically trying to keep me alive. I heard the nurse who had taken my jewelry shout, "We're losing her! We're losing her!" I turned away from the scene below me and went right through the ceiling.

It was dark, pitch black except for a small white light in the distance. As I started to move toward the light I continued to gain speed, going faster and faster. I heard voices calling out to me: "Hey...stop...help...hear me...wait...." Many of the sounds I heard were unclear. For a moment it was rather frightening...and then I was out of the tunnel and in the light. It was as if everything had come to a stop and I was in a completely different place. I sensed that there was someone on each side of me, and although I didn't look at them directly, I could see them out of the corner of my eye. There was a glow about them, and I knew they were there to help me. I believe they were angels.

As I looked around I couldn't tell where I was. In my mind's eye my body seemed to be the same, but of a much lighter density. It was as if I was, or could be, slightly transparent and there was no pain. I felt as light as air, and when I wanted to move forward, I was there. My thoughts seemed to move my body-spirit.

The next thing I noticed was a beautiful city that lay directly in front of me.

It was nestled in rolling hills and seemed to glow in radiant pastel shades of pink, yellow, blue, green and lavender. It seemed to disappear in a haze or mist in the distance, as if it were floating on a cloud. There was an unusual tall building that stood alone in the center of what appeared to be a park. It looked as if it was made of alabaster and yet it seemed to be translucent. Its contours were unusual, angling off on one side near the top. I was fascinated by its futuristic appearance...it looked like a place where records were kept. The building was surrounded by lush green lawns and beautiful flowers with a few people lovingly tending them. The beauty was beyond words, and the peace and serenity were beyond anything on earth.

Then I heard water running, and as I looked to the left I saw a gentle stream meandering through the grass. Drops of water were falling from a lovely flower onto a rock, and it made a most beautiful tinkling, musical sound. I can only describe it as angelic music, a wonderful vibration surrounding everyone, everywhere.

I wanted to get a better view of the building. I only had to think, *I wish I could see everything more clearly,* and again I moved forward without any effort on my part. It seemed as if all I had to do was think or wish something and it would happen. Suddenly my foreward movement was abruptly halted by some kind of an invisible wall.

Then I heard a voice say, "If you go any further, you cannot go back. The choice is yours." It was the voice of one of the angels, communicating telepathically. I remembered that I had communicated with them when I first arrived and how amazed I had been. Now I heard them again and I had to make a decision.

I looked at the beautiful city and I knew that as much as I wanted to stay, I would have to go back. I had work to do. Little did I know that it would be fifteen years before I realized what the work was, or why I felt I had to return to earth.

As soon as I made the decision to return to earth, I was back in my physical body on the operating table. I was aware of being in great physical discomfort and I could hear the voices of the people in the operating room. Then I lost consciousness. When I awoke I was in the recovery room and I knew my life would never be the same again.

Today that experience remains as vivid in my mind as if it happened yesterday. I believe now, just as strongly as I did then: There's nothing to fear in death. It's like being born again...only better.

In January 1986, fifteen years after my near-death experience, I started counseling people with their problems. With the heightened perceptions that came from my experience, I was able to offer hope and encouragement to those who needed it. I have studied and taught on the subject of metaphysics. It is now twelve years since I started this work and not a day goes by that someone doesn't call me for help. After all, that's where we are all supposed to do: Help one another.

I still consider every day a gift...a very precious gift.

Do you have an angel story or a mystical experience you
would like to share? If so, I would love to hear from you!
Please contact me at the following address:

JoAnne Gullickson
23233 N. Pima Road, #113-355
Scottsdale, AZ 85255

Thank you.

Do not neglect to show hospitality to strangers, for thereby some have entertained angels unawares.

—*Hebrews* 13:2 *(RSV)*